THE
INN
BOOK

THE
INN
BOOK

A FIELD GUIDE

to Old Inns & Good Food in

New York, New Jersey, Eastern Pennsylvania,

Delaware and Western Connecticut

by KATHLEEN NEUER

Drawings and Maps by EDITH SOCOLOW

THE PYNE PRESS • Princeton

First edition
Library of Congress Catalog Card Number 73-91975
SBN 87861-062-6
Printed in the United States of America
Designed by Russell Rollins

CONTENTS

INTRODUCTION

Geography Lesson

Everyone's looking around for a world that got misplaced, some-how — where there's space enough and time, where all outdoors isn't neatly plaited into belts and parkways and pushing up Colonial bent grass and Kentucky blue. How amazing to stumble on it right here in the most urbanized stretch of the most urbanized section of the country, our own maligned mid-East.

For instance, in the foothills of the Catskills there is a castle on a glacier lake in the middle of a wilderness ruled for generations by the same benign monarchical family. In the little-known tidewater country of New Jersey there's a beautiful eighteenth-century town, alive and well and as untouched as if the past 200 years had never happened. New Jerseyans have only to turn off the turnpike to reach a land as exotic as the Camargue, English countryside with horses, ghost towns as in the Golden West, forest primeval or a town made of gingerbread that sits by the sea. In certain regions of Pennsylvania you *can* go home again, for nothing has changed; Amish life is as handmade and rhythmical as it was in Biblical times. There's no love-lier valley waiting to unfold itself on a wide, wide screen than the Lehigh, crowned by the town of Bethlehem, a Moravian village at heart once you cut the steel band. The Delaware River is a glittering thread of water that shakes itself free of heavy industry north of Trenton, and strings together marvelous old river towns, romantic or seedy or sleepy by turn, and is wild as anyone could wish once you push around the bend of Port Jervis. You don't have to go all the way to Vermont to get to New England, either. Its spirit can be felt in the hills and spires of western Connecticut, and Connecticut leaves, though less well advertised, are as theatrical a backdrop as any you might find on up the road.

This is the near-country, *found* America, a look around some places we have too long overlooked.

What's in an Inn?

An inn, with or without an "e" on the end, is a slippery word, especially these days when every motel with an identity crisis calls itself one. In England the word "inn" is kept for those hostels along the road that take travelers in for the night as well as feed them, but in America an inn may do anything it jolly well chooses. (In New England the word has been used synonomously with "tavern" since Colonial days.) Most inns in this part of the world choose to provide food only; the inn-with-lodgings is an exception.

In this book, inn is used as a do-all term for many different modes of getting off the beaten path. There are farms and castles, an aging country estate, an old working grist mill, canalside taverns, even a diner, c. 1935. You'll also find a few aging belles of hotels, the term that came into general use in the mid-1800's to signify something grander than a mere dime-a-dozen inn, and grandest of all, the "house." There are also any number of "exceptions" — inns in the time-honored English tradition.

As for *restaurant*, it comes from the French "restaurer" and it means "to restore." So it should.

Eating Out as Sport

Q. *Is there really any decent food outside New York City?*

A. Yes. Decent, indecent, and on occasion food that's the equal of any to be found in the world. There's no better eating, is there, than a properly made crab cake, all crunch on the outside, lusciousness within, made with fresh lump crab and no filler? Sausage such as I didn't know existed, smoked in a little smokehouse out back, awaits in Berks County, Pennsylvania. In a lovely inn where the food had been described to me as "tearoomy," I ate a shocking lemon tart I can still taste in the roof of my mind. At a bar, an old-fashioned chocolate cake, dark, dense, and devilishly good. On a farm, just-ripened home-made vanilla ice-cream served with a mess of fresh raspberries — all you could eat.

Q. *Yes, but can you find haute cuisine?*

A. That, too, if you don't insist on defining it too closely. I remember a lovely thing with snails in a *Dijonnais* sauce, a melting rack of lamb *persillé*, an infinitely delicate veal *piccata*. I met once with the ultimate omelette. I've had things I suspect might be hard to duplicate in the city. Provencale soul food like shrimp *aïoli*. Homemade North Italian pasta. A smashing rustica pie. Boned duck, exquisitely tender, mysterious as the Orient. An English trifle that's not to be had in the whole of England. A tart of wild mushrooms – try to match *that* sometime.

Q. *But it's so expensive to eat out! How can you afford it when you're not eating on an expense account?*

A. A good way to save money is to go in the middle of the day and have lunch instead of dinner. The menu is shorter to be sure, but prices are a fraction of those later on and you get to drive back in daylight. City people report that eating out in the country *anytime* is a bargain compared to city dining.

Q. *I've been disappointed so often. Isn't it better just to stay home?*

A. Depends on the home . . . and the restaurant you have in mind. Part of the eating *art* is comparing notes. For the best odds, pick a place, if possible, where owner and chef are one, or partners, or married. Pick a small establishment – every great chef's pie-in-the-sky is a place that attempts to feed no more than sixty *maximum*. If the menu is limited to a few marvelous dishes that can be managed by the given tiny staff, take your last gallon of gas and go. All bets are off, however, if it's a Saturday night.

Q. *At those prices, am I not entitled to a little more security?*

A. Security is a dinner at Howard Johnson's, where you always know what you're getting and it's flash-frozen. In Real Life, even in capitols of gastronomy, every visit isn't going to be the great experience and every course isn't going to measure up. Think of it like plunging on tickets to a play before it opens, or April weather in Paris. A gamble. But worth it.

Q. *What about the gas problem? How do I get there from here?*

A. If you are setting out from the New York or Philadelphia area you are no more than 60 to 90 minutes away from half of the inns and regions described. The book is designed that way. The average car will take you there and back and to work the next day. Save places that are a bit further off (90-100 miles) for the weekend or a vacation and return on Monday, instead of Sunday night. Some inns are offering free stopovers that night till the pinch is over.

Consult with your innkeepers. They may have a gasoline pump on the premises or the wife's nephew may own the station. They may also provide you with other ways out—news of buses and trains to nearby points. Ask someone who doesn't drive, gas or no gas; they've learned to get around sans car, long ago.

Q. *Why didn't you use a grading system for this book—stars or forks or garbage cans?*

A. It's one way of getting you to read the text. Some inns are for eating; it's their whole raison d'être. Still other inns offer the only alternative in maybe twenty or thirty miles to a pompous food palace or a plastic motel. On one or two occasions, I've included an inn because it exudes so much charm (as distinguished from mere decor) you might willingly dispense with some of your critical faculties. Just this once.

Help Along the Road

A number of people willing to grubstake themselves in the name of gastronomy or friendship or both came along on these field trips. There isn't room to list everybody involved in this undertaking, which I hope will not be taken for ingratitude, but I would like to acknowledge at least the long-distance runners:

> Adam Blumenthal, Jack Blumenthal, Constance Bartel, Cynthia and John Eaton, Mildred and Murph Goldberger, Herbert and Phyllis Kane, Carol and Morton Klein, Betty and Howard Mele, Elizabeth Tomkins.

For kindness to a stranger:

> Jack and Linda Boucher, Adelaid and Richard Braunlich, Anne Tully and Rudy Ruderman, Jim White, Peter Fredericks.

For wine wisdom:

> Bernard DeVido, Jr., of Kingston Wines & Liquor Shop, Kingston, New Jersey.

For sharing their special expertise:

> Sue Bacchus, Joyce Countiss, Michael Dorn, Ina Gallaway, Constance Greiff, Jane Hollander, Bob Martin of the Cherry Hill *Courier Post,* Jane and Shirley Mathews of *County Magazine* in Westport, Connecticut, Elaine Tait of the Philadelphia *Inquirer,* Jess Savadge, Jean Schlesinger, Arlene Snyder.

For clues provided by these concerned members of the historical societies:

> In New Jersey—J. W. Boutellier, East Orange; Beatrice Brunswick, Burlington County; George Cotz, North Jersey Highlands; Ira D. Dorian, Cranford; Doris B. Endicott, The Friends of Ocean City Historical Museum; Edith Hoelle, Gloucester County; Louise

Jost, Monmouth County; Alice Lathrop, Marlboro Township Historical Sites and Traditions; Marilou McDonald, Morris County; Mrs. Gilbert W. Norwood, Paramus Historical and Preservation Society; B. A. Sorby, Hunterdon County.

In Pennsylvania—E. A. Kennedy, Delaware County; Richard Shultz, York County; and the Lehigh County Historical Society.

In Connecticut—Mrs. W. A. Lutz, Weston; the Ridgefield Library & Historical Association.

I.

THE HUDSON
RIVER VALLEY

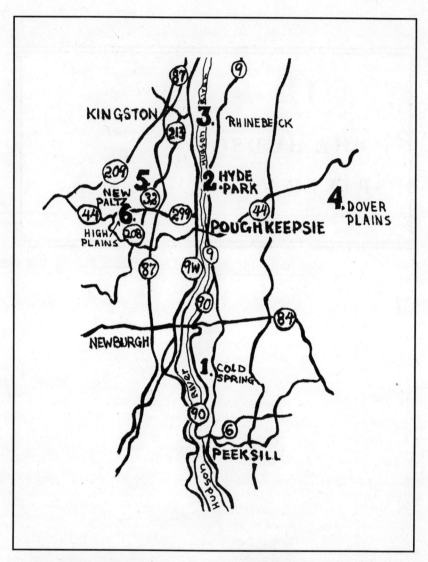

1. **HUDSON VIEW INN**
2. **THE ESCOFFIER ROOM**
3. **BEEKMAN ARMS**
4. **OLD DROVER'S INN**
5. **MOHONK MOUNTAIN HOUSE**
6. **DePUY'S CANAL (HOUSE) TAVERN**

Public transit companies serving the area: Bus from N.Y.C. — Mohawk Coach Lines (Cold Spring & Hyde Park), Short Line (Rhinebeck & New Paltz), Adirondack Trailways (New Paltz); Train from N.Y.C. — Penn-Central (Cold Spring).

EAST SIDE, WEST SIDE

About an hour this side of Albany is the center of the
world—I own it.
— Frederick Edwin Church

ONCE UPON A TIME IN AMERICA a man's home was not only his
castle, his castle was often his home. The time is the nineteenth century. The place, the Hudson River valley. On tracts of land boundless
as the sea, gentlemen of means established magnificent country seats
in the tradition of the great patroons. Everyone noted how the river
in its majesty resembled the Rhine. In the salons, partisans fought
over the relative merits of this wild shore and the old ideal provided
by Western Europe. The calm and classic backdrops appropriately
furnished with a romantic tower or an exclamation point of a cypress?
Or the lushness, the greenness, the ecstasy and excess of the still-
New World? It is not recorded who won; some might say business
interests and bulldozers, but that would not be entirely true, either.

This beautiful world-that-was, immured in money, still exists . . .
in snatches. The castles go unoccupied, but they still stand, concentrated on the east side of the river in the ninety-three miles that lie
between New York City and Rhinebeck. On the west bank are the
steep-roofed, stone houses of pre-Revolutionary days, witnesses of
an almost medieval time and place, and the gambrel-roofed Dutch
houses that form whole villages in places like New Paltz and Hurley.
On this side of the river, too, there is a wilderness that stretches out
for thousands of acres before being stopped by suburban outcroppings.
The view changes with every step of the path, from each tiny eleva-

3

tion, but you know it by heart. You've seen it before, painted by Cole, by Bierstadt, by Church and other acknowledged masters of the Hudson River school. Fortunately, nature still knows how to imitate art.

It's entirely conceivable to make the round trip in a given day with a stop-off or two and dinner on the road, but it's a large order. You would have to start early—preferably the morning *before*. A castle a day is all anyone can digest. Combine it with a picnic on the grounds when permitted or consider having lunch at one of the wineries in this region where you bring the bread and the cheese and the "thou" and purchase a jug right on the premises. THE HUDSON VALLEY WINE COMPANY in Highland, below New Paltz, looks like an idyllic wine village transplanted—grapes, buildings, bell tower and all—from the old world and set down on three hundred rolling acres high above the Hudson. A tour of the premises, accompanied by frequent wine-tastings, as well as a picnic table commanding a view of the Hudson can be had for the *prix fixe* of a dollar, the modest parking fee. On the west bank there's the BROTHERHOOD WINERY, too, near Washingtonville, America's oldest winery, located not far from SMITH'S CLOVE, a reconstructed nineteenth-century village just outside of Monroe.

In the mood for some chateau country? We have a nice chateau for you on an overlook off Route 9. French Renaissance, 65 rooms, it was first built in 1832, remodeled in 1895 by Stanford White: the OGDEN AND RUTH LIVINGSTON MILLS ESTATE in Staatsburg. In another style, the VANDERBILT MANSION, Italian Renaissance c. 1898, a short hop past the Roosevelts' place in Hyde Park. After Frederick Vanderbilt, one of the Commander's four sons, took it off the hands of John Jacob Astor, it took the services of McKim, Mead and White and $2,000,000 to make the place habitable.

If you're fond of "follies," there's LYNDHURST near Tarrytown, an American Gothic castle originally built of Sing Sing marble in the early nineteenth century and which a critic described as a folly *before* Jay Gould came into the picture, doubling the size of the house and installing his art collection. Ruins? DICK'S CASTLE on Route 9D high on a hilltop near Garrison, an American Alhambra begun in 1905 and abandoned $3,000,000 later for lack of funds. Vandalized without mercy, it's somewhat restored now and made into an industrial museum. The wildly romantic OLANA, home of the Hudson River landscape artist Frederick Edwin Church, is a Moorish extravaganza he built for himself, the culmination of his travels. It overlooks the Hudson in the town of Hudson above Rhinebeck. For more individualism rampant, SUNNYSIDE near Tarrytown, writer-diplomat Washington Irving's improvisations on a saltbox, is a sheer delight. BOSCOBEL in Garrison, the apogee of a Robert Adams villa, is States Dyckman's "last sacrifice to Folly," and exquisite in every spare-no-expense detail. Sold to a wrecker for $35, it has been restored with astonishing grace and fidelity, using many of the original furnishings, and embellished with a *son et lumiere* show.

The Dutch patroons lived like lords on feudal fiefs. Frederick Philipse, master builder, the wealthiest man in the colonies and a millionaire before the word was coined, owned 86,000 acres in Westchester. He built the PHiLIPSE MANOR in the virgin territory that is now downtown Yonkers in 1682, and further north in Tarrytown, a manor on the Pocantico River that became a trading center under his son – PHILLIPSBURG MANOR.

The VAN CORTLANDT HOUSE in Croton-on-the-Hudson is a grand-manner manor, a mirror of the changing styles and tastes of this powerful family. As operators of the ferry they were required to maintain a ferry house and kitchen which is also on view.

The Roosevelts of HYDE PARK lived very well, too. Their family place with its mementos of the President, boy and man, and the library built six years before he died, is a prime tourist magnet. Franklin and Eleanor, immune to the recent stormy revelations of their troubled marriage, lie side by side in the rose garden.*

At Cold Spring the river is not at arm's length, to be viewed from some high promontory, but right at the end of the road where a covered pavilion is silhouetted against the dazzle. There are benches about on the mossy green banks that go down to the water, and just across the street you'll find the second oldest inn in New York (so the legend on the menu goes):

*For a more complete listing write the Hudson River Valley Association, 105 Ferris Lane, Poughkeepsie, New York 12603.

HUDSON VIEW INN
Cold Spring

ON A NICE DAY if you work it right, you could sit in the sun on the tiny terrace in front and sip raspberry beer – Berliner weisse. This is a beer partially fermented right in the bottle and poured (there's a trick to the pouring) over a great stain of raspberry purée. You try it because you don't find raspberry beer very often this side of Berlin 1, and 2, it's delicious, a fascinating paradox of flavors. If you feel such overripe pleasures helped bring about the downfall of Germany, have a stein of Späten brau, the beautiful Munich beer, or, for the peasants, Löwenbräu, light and dark, all on tap.

The beer gets the food it deserves, the big resounding chords of German cooking, the *schnitzels*, the *sauerbraten*, the *knockwurst*, the dumplings, the *winekraut*. The *schnitzel* made with milk-fed veal is so light it hardly touches the plate. Fish is fresh, swimming upstream every day from the Fulton fish market and prepared in honest and interesting ways. Homemade *strudel* bulges with cheese or cherries.

The bar is a flea market of pop art and useless objects, from the shell-encrusted African ceremonial spear over the door to autographed cocktail coasters (Frank and Lee-Ann, Doris and Del) on the walls. It looks lived-in, it *is* lived-in, continuously since 1837. The sandwiches served here can easily pinch-hit for a meal or a meal-and-a-half. Platter-size rounds of buttered rye or pumpernickel are stuffed and *over*stuffed with Krakus ham or roast top sirloin or Genoa salami, helped along with potato salad, pickles, lettuce and tomatoes.

The food is good, yes. It *should* be with the former Luchow maitre d' and his wife running things. Sunday dinner is rated G (for the whole family). Afterwards save time to explore the village where there is a better than usual collection of antique shops.

Hudson View Inn, *Cold Spring-on-Hudson, N.Y. 10616. Marie-Louise Link, Prop. L – noon-2:30, D – 5.30-9 Tues., Wed. & Thurs., till 9.30 Fri. & Sat., noon-8 Sunday. Sandwiches, snacks always available. Closed Mon. except some legal holidays, month of Jan. Phone: 914-265-3625.*

The smells that greet you when you enter this formidable chateau on the Hudson are the same tell-tale school smells found anywhere in America, a compound of sneaker scuffs-on-tile and pencil shavings and exhausted air. Yet down these halls lies your destination, the most ambitious restaurant in the entire valley:

THE ESCOFFIER ROOM
Culinary Institute of America
Hyde Park, New York

WHATEVER CRUMBS of hope there are to save gastronomy in this country is based largely on this college where young barbarians go cold turkey on the ketchup for two years while they learn to cook as well as comprehend menu-French. Student waiters must also learn other things like controlling facial muscles . . . fencing with serving implements . . . fire-fighting at tableside. For the dining room is formal, forgives nothing. That glorious silver carving cart? A legacy from Le Pavillion. At each well-laid table, a long-stemmed rose shoots sharply upward. Balloon glasses yawn, demand wine. Chairs are leather, throne-like. The place is a veritable museum of tradition. (If all you had in mind was a melted cheese, there's a first rate diner on the grounds.)

The menu which is changed every two weeks is, in a word, flabbergasting. It dips at will into the best the world has to offer and damn the expense (labor, at least, is not a factor). Roast wild boar . . . pressed duck . . . Canadian salmon . . . capon with truffles . . . *contrefilet de boeuf.* Nor is it bound by the dictates of French cuisine alone. Besides Spanish, Italian, Swedish, Indian, Near-Eastern on the current bill-of-fare, there is a strong infusion of Chinese which makes itself felt not only in such items as the exquisite Pong Pong chicken (morsels of chicken in a complicated Szechuan sauce involving peanuts) but spills over into other cuisines as well. If the delightful *gnocchi verde* described as "A regional Italian dish . . . tiny dumplings prepared from a commixture of chicken, spinach and potato etc." has a touch of greatness it may be a secret Chinese weapon called waterchestnuts chopped exceedingly fine to add a mysterious texture.

The three-course lunch, served with hot homemade rye rolls and baby croissants, and followed with a luxurious pecan bar — lagniappe — is $7.50; the five-course dinner, $14.50.

The adjoining Rabelais bar has a window wall looking in on the kitchen where the intricacies of the menu are worked out before a gallery of eyes. Since the chef is ill, a sous-chef is in charge under the eye of the director. Like any good repertory theater, the show goes on, without stumbling, without stars, while school's in session.

The Escoffier Room, *Culinary Institute of America, Rte. 9, Hyde Park, N.Y. L — 12-2.30 Mon.-Fri., D — 6-8.30 Mon.-Sat. Closed Sun. and open irregularly during semester breaks and school holidays. Check by phone: 914-471-6608.*

The minute you go south of New England, the traditional inn-with-lodging grows scarcer and scarcer, but there are a few. One is a hotel said to be the oldest in America —

BEEKMAN ARMS
Rhinebeck, New York

FRANKLIN DELANO ROOSEVELT, who lived just down the road at *Hyde Park*, used to wind up all his many campaigns at these premises. Theodore Roosevelt before him was a visitor. William Jennings Bryan orated from a second-floor window, and Horace Greeley was a frequent guest. General Washington and his staff bided a while here, and soldiers for the Revolution were trained on the lawn next door. Beekman Arms goes back to the founding of Rhinebeck in 1715 when refugees from the Palatinate resettled on the American Rhine and this inn served as town hall, Sunday meeting place, redoubt and refuge. In the next fifty years it expanded into roughly the building you find at the core today.

The effluvia of the past is still powerful enough to overshadow the latest expansions and the ceaseless hustle (a wedding is scheduled to take place here on the following day). The scattered, scarred antiques in the lobby, old weaponry mounted on beams, a huddle of wing chairs about the fire, old pewter highlights and grandfather clocks help furnish memories. Upstairs there are candles in the rooms for romantics who want to turn back the clock, if only for a night. A pitcher and bowl are placed outside the bathroom presumably for the same reason.

The chef who is reputed to hail from the Culinary Institute down the road, pleases a lot of people a lot of the time, to judge by the crowds. Still it is doubtful that he got more than a "B" on his beef Stroganoff; and waitresses in mob caps weren't designed to bring forth desserts like *Jean La Fite* (coffee with cognac and chocolate ice cream — the ice cream, instantly melted by the coffee, adds nothing but its chill). Stick to uncomplicated broiler items, stick to ribs, and you'll be all right.

If you like to go to sleep before midnight make sure your room is on the third floor. If you don't, join the festivities in the taproom, which has been going non-stop now for nearly three hundred years.

Before leaving town take a walking tour of RHINEBECK, a living textbook of early American architectural styles, and a side trip to the pretty village of RHINECLIFF. Across the river is KINGSTON and a little farther the old stone village of HURLEY. For another kind of glance back, visit the OLD RHINEBECK AERODROME with its collection of early flying machines. On weekends in the summer against all the odds they hold a rendezvous in the sky while you hold your breath — *this is no movie.*

> Beekman Arms, *Rhinebeck, N.Y. 12572. Charles La Forge, Prop. L—noon-3 Mon.-Fri., D—5-10 Mon.-Sat., noon-9 Sun. Closed Christmas.* Lodgings. *Phone: 914-876-7077.*

In certain unyoung and old-moneyed circles it's a kind of litany, how nowhere is as good as it was forty, twenty, even fifteen years ago when they first went there, nothing, and they go down the list. Heads shake. Hands shake as a drink is raised. You begin to feel quite blue till you mull it over and exceptions leap to mind, like the Jersey shore before mosquito control, like the luxurious

OLD DROVER'S INN
Dover Plains, New York

WHAT WOULD those New England cowboys say, the cattle drovers, who used to drive the herds to market down the Old Post Road, down the years from the mid-seventeenth to mid-eighteenth centuries, and stop for a night of wheeling and dealing and drinking at what used to be called Clear Water Tavern? Outwardly the old place peering out under the trees looks much the same except for two black Rolls and one taupe Bentley in the driveway. The firewood is leaning up against the house on the long covered portico as before. The stone walled taproom with a fire twisting and turning in the hearth hasn't changed either, really. A little wearier. A lot less bloody. The gaming tables are gone, long since replaced by *The Wall Street Journal.* Nobody is downing mulled ale.

Upstairs, though, it's another country, a country of umbrella stands and barometers and fat little cushions – goose down. Someone must do nothing but go around plumping them, plumping them. Off the eighteenth-century drawing room is the library panelled in books chosen with the same deliberation as the porcelains – Jane Austen, Jean Genet, Sir Winston, *Larousse Gastronomique* – chosen, you can't help feeling, for their sizes and colors and shapes as much as their insides. An *Oxford Universal Dictionary* is open on a stand. Off the other end of the drawing room, the beautiful Federal breakfast room with its Georgian candelabra and its polished mahogany, with its scenes of the surrounding countryside (Hyde Park . . . West Point . . . Old Drover's itself) painted by Edward Paine.

Up more stairs to the guest chambers, rooms with shadows and ghosts and fireplaces and a collector's choice of fine old antiques. Six in all, no two are alike. The Meeting Room, so-called, was once a gathering place for the townspeople; under the arched ceiling are two splendid spool beds, each double-size, two writing desks and two wing chairs brooding before the fireplace. In the Sleigh Room, a leather-clad wing chair, an early Empire chest, a needlepoint footstool on the hooked rug, and a sleigh bed of darkest mahogany. Each bed has its velvet-covered down quilt folded, *so*, into an inverted butterfly and placed at the foot; when the chill comes on in the predawn hours, a mere touch and you're covered – no need to wake up. There are your bags, someone has brought them, unasked. Someone has set the fire in the hearth. The same someone will steal back later, before you retire, and light it. He'll also turn down the sheets and inquire when you take breakfast and if you'd like a look at *The New York Times* with your coffee or–? It begins to feel like normalcy and all the rest of living a terrible hardship, a bad dream.

Strangers at the next banquette watch closely as the waiter produces your drink – Lillet with a twist of orange peel sloshing around in a 15-ounce tumbler – just to see the reaction they admit, coddling their second 15-ounce vodka martinis. Stuffed eggs, a specialty, is more largesse. Skinker Travis Harris all in black leather (perhaps to match his shiny Rolls) hangs the menu-on-a-slate from the nearest beam. Steak and kidney pie, shrimp rarebit, curry – all long-standing traditions – beckon, but your pointer stops at Chukka partridge. (Later you learn the birds are raised to order by a neighbor down the road.) Served with a wild rice stuffing and a currant-and-red-wine sauce, it's quite contenting. A popover comes by, hot, ambushed in a napkin, an old weakness. By now you have stopped regretting the thin, meaningless lemon soup—anyone knows the cheddar cheese soup is the soup to have here, since it is supposed to have originated on this spot. You plan on another popover but it never materializes. Instead, dessert—Key Lime pie and it's the genuine article with the right amount of wry.

Much of the ambiance in the taproom comes from the shimmer of overblown hurricanes of etched glass. "Lots of people seem to like them," the bartender says modestly, "so we have the person who makes them for us make some up for our guests. They're $350 a pair—" Unlike the missing Boehm pheasant ($1000) and the Woolworth glass ashtrays, they're too large to smuggle out as a souvenir.

Ten, twenty years from now, if you're around playing you-should-have-been-here-when, it's the breakfast above all you're likely to remember and recount. The dead-ripe slices of honeydew with a crescent of lime. The inn's own blueberry griddle cakes served with melted butter and hot maple syrup side by side in their pitchers . . . served with sausage patties cooked precisely as directed—"crisp in the *middle*." (Why shouldn't they be good, made up as they are to Old Drover specifications by a sausage-maker in the city?) And coffee, a steady stream from silver pot to porcelain cup, *gorgeous* coffee. If $7.50 for breakfast is a bit much to swallow, you could settle for the *continental* breakfast, $3.00, or have the same meal for *lunch* at $1.50 more.

The present owner, a nephew of the founder, is said to be a rich man and he spends a lot of time here. This is a place where the rich can come and feel wanted. Isn't it high time some of the rest of us learn how the other half lives, if only for a day?

> Old Drover's Inn, *Old Drover's Inn Rd., Dover Plains, N.Y. 12522. Located 12 mi. N of Pawling on Rte. 22. James E. Potter, Prop. L—noon-3, D—6-9 weekdays, noon-9.30 Sat., 1-8.30 Sun. Closed Tues. & Wed.—also 3 weeks in Dec.* Lodgings. *Reservations imperative Sat. evening:* 914-832-3811.

THE CARRIAGES AND SLEIGHS that used to meet the train at New Paltz in the '80's are still the only vehicles permitted on the roads. Until quite recently they even fetched guests from the gatehouse two and a half miles below, carrying them up, up to a cliff house with uncounted turrets, chimneys, gables, and balconies that seems to take form out of the same sheared rock that rings the lake. You feel as if you've come to a small country in Europe or maybe it's Canada— Banff, but you are only an hour-and-a-half from New York at

MOHONK HOUSE
New Paltz, New York

CIVILIZATION-AS-WE-KNEW-IT is making a stubborn stand for survival at Mohonk. Impertinent motorcars and developers are kept at bay by a wilderness preserve of over 7,500 acres, one-fifth of the Shawangunk Mountains in Ulster County. (These mountains, pronounced unpronounceably *Shon-gum*, parallel the Catskills to the north.)

If you want to penetrate more deeply than is possible by carriage or on horseback it is imperative that you walk. At Mohonk *everybody* walks. There are 110 miles of paths and trails. Mountain, forest stream, green glacial lake, aloof escarpment, misty valley, giant rock garden are led up to and revealed with bravura by masters of nineteenth-century landscape art who were, to say the least, great showmen. Silvery thatch-roofed gazebos, almost Japanese, are planted seductively in front of one or another masterpiece of this open-air gallery, and from one point you can see five states at a glance. If all this sounds too civilized for your taste, you might apply to Mohonk for permission to climb the TRAPPS, the most ambitious rock-climbing area in all the East.

The "house" has grown from ten guest rooms in 1870 to 300 but it remains comfortable and familiar somehow—a house is not a hotel! One hundred and fifty rooms have fireplaces; when you need more firewood you summon it forth with a bell. There is much dark wainscoting, dun colors, golden oak—Mohonk is masculine rather than feminine Victorian—and no one has the effrontery to tamper with things, mercifully. There's space to burn, particularly the elegant 60' long parlour wing built out over the lake on trusses, much admired by architecture critic Ada Louise Huxtable. Passing out to the porch, glance down over the railing to see fat, rosy-flanked trout tame as seals swimming in place below—it must be tea time.

There are no rules at Mohonk House but "woe to you if you break one." This castle-crowned principality on a mountaintop was completely self-sufficient until a few years ago and has been under the governance of the same Quaker family, the Smileys, for four generations. They have their little ways, the Smileys. Three years ago they relented the rules to permit polite drinking in the rooms, where ice and set-ups will be brought, and in the dining room during the preprandial hour. But why not take tea instead served at four in the Main Lounge? Or have yourself a soda in the old-fashioned ice cream parlour? Naturally there's no smoking in the dining room or parlour—nice people don't pollute. Telephones are confined to the halls where they are planted on rockers. As for television—who needs television when almost any evening there are slide shows in the lounge.

An unusual family. Some years ago they refused to resort to sprays to fend off the predations of the gypsy moth and lo! they still have their trees. David Smiley always carries a portable vacuum cleaner with him and wisks it out on his field trips. Soprano Virginia Smiley sings like a bird, literally, and often performs when she takes groups out birdwatching. If anyone can help you sort out what a brochure calls "the confusing fall warblers," she can. Rachel Smiley rises each day at 5:30 to fill the hotel with flowers. Her husband, Ben Matteson, a v.p., is the kind of man who refuses to exile the maraschino cherry since he can find no evidence of wrongdoing on the label; he stands firm even in the teeth of an invasion by the natural food people who, like Joseph Buonoparte, are bringing their own chef. A lower administrative vassel puts his head in the v.p.'s door: "Getting the vegetarian count now," he says, and ducks out.

When walking and birdwatching palls, there are other ways to spend the time. Swimming in the lake (there's a crescent of sand and a large floating raft for sunners) . . . peddle- and row-boating . . . tennis and golf and putting. In winter, sleigh-riding, snowshoeing, cross-country skiing and even some downhill (a 475' downhill run with a rope tow). For restless types, there's the hushed Huguenot houses of NEW PALTZ nearby, and LAKE MINNESWAWSKA, a former Smiley pro-tectorate with *two* cliff houses poised on a blue-eyed-blue glacier lake. See them before they join the rest of lost America, for they're slated some day soon to be replaced by an Edward Durrell Stone palace.

And there's eating.

To get to the dining room you pass in review before a gallery of for-mer guests, blackbeards, greybeards, with twinkly or judgmental eyes who look at very least like Vice-President what's-his-name or Andrew Carnegie. Some of them *were* Andrew Carnegie. Also Sir Wilfred Grenfell and John Burroughs. Four were Presidents. Eminent Vic-torians all.

Lunch is a buffet with something for everybody.* By carefully weaving in and out you may locate old-fashioned chicken and dump-lings, *bratwurst* and hot German potato salad and – skipping the jel-lied fruit molds – a bottomless bowl of greens, another of the reddest ripest tomatoes, another of thinnest sliced purple onions. Here's *cold* potato salad and the usual litany of relishes. Here's ears of corn delivered up from watery depths hot and dripping. Poached fresh salmon disappoints (Mohonk fans agree fish is not understood here) but chicken and dumplings like this, with great chunks of white meat and bouffant dumplings in a sauce that's the essence of chicken, makes up for it. It's simply, unstylishly great. The baking, done on the premises, is astonishingly good: tenderest, flakiest falling-apart Napoleons, a fine hazelnut torte with marzipan icing, a double-dark chocolate confection-of-a-cake, éclairs – the superior little ones – and more. Most diners help themselves to two desserts, scurrying back to their tables in the vast golden oak reaches of the dining room like naughty children. They needn't . . . nobody sees or cares.

The waitress who, like so many of the waitresses on the premises, looks like a solemn English nanny approaches and asks what you'll have to drink.

You tell her, but she remains standing.

Tea, please, you repeat with more conviction, and after another pause, when she doesn't stir, ask: Is there something wrong?

No, no, she says quickly, businesslike, a bit aggrieved. You didn't

---

*Many guests come just for the lunch ($6.50) and to spend the day, helping themselves to the grounds. The day guest fee alone is $5.

tell me what *kind*—English Breakfast or Earl Grey or Oolong or Mohonk Darjeeling?

> Mohonk Mountain House, *New Paltz, N.Y. 12561. Located 6 mi. W of New Paltz. The Smiley Bros., Prop. Open daily year-round. L—12.30-2, till 2.30 Sat. & Sun., D— 6.30-8.30. Lodgings & bkfst. Bus, train, plane & limousine connections available. Reservations imperative: 914-255-1000.*

Down the mountain a piece from Mohonk there used to be a canal to transport coal from Pennsylvania to New York, abandoned after the turn of the century and filled with detritus. Young canal-buff John Novi passed it every day—the town is very small—and dreamed about restoring it and the boarded-up bargeman's tavern alongside. As soon as he came of age he borrowed money and bought

DePUY'S CANAL TAVERN
High Plains, New York

A Mohonk official shook his close-cropped head when discussing DePuy's. The food, yes, is extraordinary, though of course he wouldn't want to eat there every night. But he worries about John (Novi). He's such a dreamer—.

Novi, on the other hand, who married his wife under a Mohonk gazebo on a Mohonk mountain, is worried about the future of *Mohonk*, of changes that threaten it in the name of "business."

The dreamer was just twenty-one when he bought Simeon DePuy's (duh-pewz) old place nearly a decade ago now. Then, like any athlete, he went into training, taking himself to Europe to learn how to cook and serve. He ate well too, splurging frequently at good tables, and understood what he ate, a very important part of the training. When he returned he opened his restaurant and eight months later made history himself when food editor and restaurant critic Craig Claiborne and some friends (friends like the former chef of General Charles de Gaulle) dropped in. The report in *The New York Times* was decorated with four stars. Does this mean, as it so often means, a kind of permission to go downhill ever after? Not if, like Novi, you're a virtuoso and this is the way you perform. He performs so well he created a kind of viewing stand on the second floor overlooking the kitchen; anyone who cares to may climb up and watch—cooking as spectator sport.

Tonight is the debut of a whole new menu. Every season the menu, kept wisely to four choices, is changed—you could almost say scored— and set forth in a spidery hand on a slate. Not one item is a cliché, or anything you're likely to encounter ever again unless you go home with the recipe in hand. If a menu can be **too** interesting, this one is—starting with, compliments of the house, an absolutely astonishing pop-in-mouth cream puff filled with a cherry tomato and a heavenly mayonnaise. If you order the *rustica* pie, the Sicilian pudding pie made with ricotta and eggs and sausage bits which is a major glory of this restaurant, you must forego finding out what a raw fish-and-avocado-appetizer tastes like, perhaps forever. The tyranny of decisions! All right, let's say not eating raw fish is not your problem. What about the entrées? The fresh tuna in a pesto sauce (garlic-basil paste), a culinary **event** according to reports, means passing up *filet of beef Toklas à la De Puy en croûte*—a beef Wellington like no one's else. This masterpiece-in-progress, marinated a bit overlong on its debut night, is served up beautifully and *much* too generously, nonetheless, with a veritable dance of zucchini *frites*, each one **placed** on the plate, **so**. The *gabladini,* an Italian vegetable stew involving eggplant, mushrooms, capers, coming on top of it is too much, admittedly, but you eat it all for you don't find *gabladini's* at every Kentucky Fried Chicken. Salad, then a bowl of magazine-illustration fruit and a vast tray of mellowed cheeses follow. A weak nod to it all—the *riccota salata*, one purple grape, and a pear. Desserts are merciless. Cheesecake or an extraordinary chocolate cake in three textures or éclairs or Bird's Nest pudding (made with apple) are ranged with three dark red chrysanthemums on the dessert tray. The wise will point to the chrysanthemums.

Soon there will be lodgings nearby for you to take refuge in, owned and operated by some of the same people who bring you escarole egg drop soup and prime rib *portmanteau*. Novi and friends are communards in some ways; three waiters have been here since '69 when the restaurant opened. Meanwhile, if you want to stay overnight, there is an old brick house down the road owned by a tiny woman of eighty-six years who welcomes any friends of the Novi's, and of course Mohonk House nearby which allows a modest deduction on the bill when you notify them of your intentions to eat out.

There is a standing offer to take you on a tour after dinner. **Go.** The place and everything in it is a delight, from end to end, upstairs and down and down some more to the basement where the canal mules used to be sheltered. The latter is being turned into a cafe where a more modest supper-on-a-tray will be available. Out in back the canal and its five locks have been dug out, freed at last from their long, long sleep.

DePuy Canal (House) Tavern, *Rte. 213, High Falls, N.Y. 12440. John P. Novi, Prop. Located a few miles NW of New Paltz — directions forthcoming when you make your reservation (essential). D — 5.30-10 Thurs., Fri., Sat., 3-9 Sun. Closed Mon, Tues. & Wed. Phone: 914-687-7700.*

II.

CONNECTICUT—
NEW ENGLAND-
NEXT-DOOR

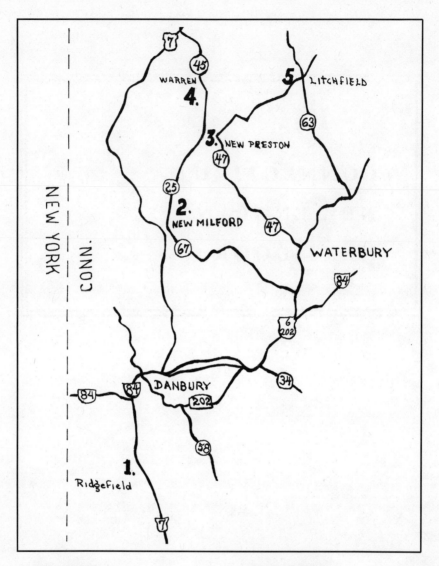

1. **THE ELMS**
2. **YOUNG'S HOTEL**
3. **HOPKINS INN**

4. **L'HERMITAGE**
5. **KILVAROOK INN**

Public transit companies serving the area: Bus from N.Y.C.—Greyhound (Ridgefield, New Milford, New Preston, Litchfield), Bonanza (Ridgefield).

EVERYONE KNOWS what a proper New England inn looks like. The white house with the dark shutters, the waiting porch and its petunias, the welcome. You could draw a floor plan with your eyes shut and put the chimneys in all the right places. The same is even truer of the village with its church and steeple, Main Street with its overhang of trees and houses set well back each on its appointed green. Such airy models are hard to match in the real world but there's one that answers the description and it's called

THE ELMS INN
Ridgefield, Connecticut

OVERLAID on all that New England dignity is still another tradition even older. European *politesse*, it might be called. The Elms is another success story for the melting pot. The two traditions work together for the guest who gets the best of both worlds.

The parlour is Victorian, the taproom pure Colonial and the guest rooms upstairs with their fourposters and carved dressers and hooked rugs Attic Antique. The inn was built in 1760, but when you cross the threshold of the dining room you're back in the old world, a world upheld by standards and surrounded, cocooned, by the tradition of service. Clues are all over the place. The fresh flowers, the even fresher daffodil linen. Fresh fragile breadsticks still warm from the oven instead of cellophane-wrapped crackers. The wine, the ordi-

21

nary house wine chilled to the bone, glass and all (and 3000 more well-chosen bottles stashed below in the cellar). Pâté is brought forth potted, iced in chicken fat, served with toast points – so good it's not quite real. (The pâté is famous in this neighborhood and makes all the best parties though quite expensive at $6 for one-half pound. On the premises it's just $.50!) The lunch menu includes such dishes as *omelette Périgourdine* (with truffles), *steak tartare, turbot bonne femme,* poached salmon with green mayonnaise and most exotic of all, braised chicory, the day's vegetable. For dinner there are veal racks as well as lamb racks, scampi, *steak au poivre,* and, quite frequently, game. Quail, when found on these preserves, is a buy – $10.75 on the table d'hote Sunday dinner. *Fettucini Alfredo* may be ordered à la carte. Desserts are mostly ice cream in one good guise or another with a pear Burgundy here, cheese-and-crackers there and *crêpes suzettes* for celebrants.

The Elms is a local institution. Over the years it has maintained itself in the affection and esteem of the local population, a worldly bunch, but it's much too good to keep for the natives.

> The Elms Inn, 500 *Main St., Ridgefield, Conn. 06877. Near the center of town (Rte. 35). Marlo & Robert Scala, Prop. L – noon-2.30, D – 6-9.30, noon-10 Sat., 1-8.30 Sun. Closed Wed. & Mar. or April for vacation.* Lodgings. *AE, BA, DC, MC. For reservations: 203-438-2541.*

In New England the leaves start turning a good three weeks earlier than they do just one hundred miles south, say around the New York àrea. If you're coming, come early and catch them in the act. . . . Or plan a trip in the spring. After you've said goodby to the lilacs, and the cherry blossoms are a memory in the grass, head north and catch the rerun. Either way, if you plan it right, manage to be in New Milford in time to have lunch down by the railroad tracks at,

YOUNG'S HOTEL
New Milford, Connecticut

THIS OLD BATTERED HOTEL, a survivor of the decline and fall of the railroad, was kept from total decay when a former policeman, Edward Dyer, bought it and brought it back to respectability by the honesty of its food and the drawing power of an honorable old bar. Made it not only respectable but even a kind of magnet for people in the area – storekeepers, artists, clerks, gentry.

The secret ingredient of Young's success is the fish. Half the menu (the *important* half) is given over to fish and seafood and it couldn't be fresher if New Preston were smack on the Sound. It's simply prepared, grilled for the most part, and served on a sizzling plank. With fish this fresh, it's all that's required. If you know what month it is you can pretty much guess what's on the menu. February through April, shad and roe . . . May, June, softshells, available sautéed if you ask nicely . . . September through April, it's open season on oysters which may be had deep-fried or, on request, stewed. This day, bluefish is quite a catch at $1.75 along with a homemade clam chowder, a splash of mashed potatoes and an order of cole slaw. For non-fish-eaters there's the usual pork chops and baked hams and an unusual $5.50 Porterhouse and an acclaimed chopped steak. For non-meat-eaters who don't touch fish, there's the Pegeen Fitzgerald vegetable plate. Is everybody happy?

Desserts get short shrift, but there is pie around (no longer homemade as claimed) and biscuit strawberry shortcake (unavailable on this visit) if you don't want ice cream or jello or tapioca pudding. In the fall hold off and buy glorious crackling apples by the side of the road.

> Young's Hotel, *10 Railroad St., New Milford, Conn. 06776.*
> *Located 12 mi. N of Danbury (Rtes. 7 & 25 . . . make rt. at*
> *Veteran's Bridge). Richard Kajikawa, Acting Mgr. & Chef.*
> *L – 11.30-2; D – 5-9, noon-7.30 Sun. Phone: 203-354-7906.*

New Preston which is just off Route 25 north of New Milford has a church with a steeple, a pavilion hall, a hardware store, a drug store, a grocery store stockpiled with scandal sheets and bubble gum, and a barber shop reeking of bay rum – two of nothing – and at the backdoor, a three-mile lake. Contoured by a ring of hills, the lake is prettier than most. It has swimming at one end and a state-run park at the other, power boats and sailboats and ducks, and it has the loveable

---

HOPKINS INN

New Preston, Connecticut

THOSE TWO splendid silvery people sitting in pomp on the Victorian sofa in the back parlour have been everywhere and done everything and now in their eighties they come *every night* from May to November to have dinner at the inn, though their home is over twenty miles away. They are here in the summer when dinner is served under the trees on the patio while the sun eventually dissolves in the lake and the moon materializes in the sky and through the fall when fires are set to leaping in room after room and diners draw up with an aperitif or after-dinner coffee or cognac as if guests in their own home.

"Why go elsewhere?" the couple-who-have-been-everywhere ask, "it is all *here – right here.*"

As a kind of recognition of fealty the P——'s have been made godparents of Nicole, the innkeepers' daughter. And Nicole is certainly here, lunging tirelessly after the doorstep kitten who was smuggled in under the coatjacket of an errant guest. She stops to accept a pretzel from her godfather but when *"bitte"* is demanded, sidesteps, diving for the bowl. Nicole's mother hooks her deftly by the sashtails as she sets down a tray of drinks. Exit Nicole. Margrit Hilfiker returns, pressing forward a pretty young woman in white waitress' uniform, and asking, "May Ernestine eat with you tonight? She helps us out on busy nights but tonight is rather quiet and she has driven all the way out here for nothing –." "Certainly, certainly," the couple nod approvingly. "You see the kind of place this is!" asks the beautiful, imperious Mrs. P —— rhetorically.

Hopkins Place was purchased directly from the Indians in 1781 by Elijah Hopkins whose great-great grandson opened the inn, whose descendants still own and work the farm next door. The building sits tall on a rise above the lake, a three-story yellow frame house surmounted by a cupola. It was built in the early 1800's, added to from time to time, but judiciously. The great Swiss showman and chef, Albert Stockli, who shook the world at Stonehenge in Connecticut and masterminded Restaurant Associates' Four Seasons (in New York City), found Hopkins Inn for the Hilfiker's. Swiss-schooled Rudy

Hilfiker, who used to train staff for places like Stonehenge, abetted by two Swiss trainees in his own kitchen, is performing small miracles every day, twice a day. A shrimp bisque that is the essence of shrimp-ness. A *piccata Milanese* heaped with mushrooms and ham out of the kind of pink-pearl veal that is often said to be unprocurable in the United States. A round of dense white bread with knife plunged in its heart has to be homemade (it is). The "vins du pays" is Fendant de Sion (there's also a Dezaley and a red Dole, the Swiss stars) and arrives with all due pomp, up to the neck in ice. Rum *babas* are homemade that very afternoon. Espresso, as is always true for some reason in Switzerland, is a supreme experience.

Regulars at Hopkins are spoiled **regularly**, can wheedle treats like garlicky tripe stew and homely peasant dishes reserved for "family." One fan in the neighborhood never has anything but calves' brains *au buerre noir* on or off the menu.

The best guest rooms are at the front of the house overlooking the water. They're simply furnished, summery rooms with an occasional old piece, and splashes of sunlight. Despite lapses into cuteness (a hex bar with an actual Hopkins tombstone in the floor . . . a display of "antique" hats in the hall) there is an absence of chic, an innocence that refreshes eye and heart. And there's the lake. You can swim in it, sail on it, ski on it, or watch silently while the light plays over it, repainting it hourly. When that palls, strike up the road – any road – and you're deep in country. LITCHFIELD-the-beautiful is just twenty minutes away. Switzerland is right here.

> Hopkins Inn, *Lake Waramaug, New Preston, Conn. 06777. Located a little past the village of New Preston (follow signs to the inn). Margaret & Rudolf Hilfiker, Prop. L – noon-2 Tues.-Sat.; D – 6-9 Tues.-Fri., till 9.30 Sat., 1-3, 5-8 Sun. Closed Mon. Open May thru Oct. Lodgings, breakfast avilable. Sat. reservations needed: 203-868-7295.*

A native son of Litchfield who moved out of state long since laughed chokingly when asked to recommend a restaurant in the area; to think of eating well in the country of his boyhood struck his funnybone. In those corners of the world where meals are considered little more than an obstacle in the day and eating well bad for the character, they get, it seems, the food they deserve.

But the area has changed. The old guard is leaving, new people "from the Valley" are moving in, summer people are staying, and the ascetic ideal has lost its cutting edge, its nobility. Cucumber sandwiches, delicious as they may be, are no longer enough. It was inevitable that a missionary or two move in After the Fall to bring *La Gratinée des Halles* to the land of floury clam chowder. Now native sons and daughters can go home again without facing a winter of starva-

tion. Le Pavillion has come to this corner of Connecticut and it goes
under the name of

L'HERMITAGE

Warren, Connecticut

ONCE YOU GET to the village it's easy to find. Look for the witches'
hat of a steeple atop the church on the hill, a famous landmark, and go
the other way. Warren itself is a dot along the Connecticut back
roads, known these days as the home of artist Eric Sloane.

The glorious ruddy sugar maple in front of the two-hundred-year-
old farmhouse was a tree to be reckoned with before the house was
built. Lit from above by a harvest moon and below by newly-installed
bubble lights, it appears to be consuming itself. Inside there is no
future for nostalgia. All is calm, is monastic, is white, extraneous
décor declared out of bounds. Janine or Marcel greet you, barely.
(Le Pavillion has exported more than a former captain and wife; it
has choreographed the faint chill of welcome, the split-second smile.
Eating – you had forgotten, perhaps? – is serious business.) A woman
alone on a Saturday night is not necessarily a *bad* woman so much as
a non-person. Don't be ruffled. Even a male companion at your side
would not produce the longed-for result, a whisper in the ear from the
heavy-lidded waiter as he flicks a napkin at a non-existent ash: "Dover
sole is a no-no." The cheese-spread in front of you that tastes like a
bride's first dip tells you nothing and what would Soulé say to these
salty cellophaned crackers? "What do you recommend, Marcel?" Marcel is tableside . "*Riz de Veau Toulouse Lautrec,*" be comes back without missing a beat, pencil poised. "What about the bass '*a la façon du
chef*'?" "Take the *riz de Veau,*" he replies. "– the *Canard croustil-
lant aux peches? Pigeon à la mir –?*" "*Riz de Veau.*" The man is
adamant. The pencil has been waiting a long time. You nod and sen-
tence is passed.

A large, beautifully pruned artichoke is set before you like a bouquet, with a well of creamy vinaigrette within, a perfect thing. It takes
several hours to eat it all, but once launched on this journey, it's impossible to stop. (The same dressing reappears later on a salad of
watercress and romaine.) Only with difficulty can you convey the
fact that you'd like to order wine; perhaps the waiter has heard how
artichokes make wines taste sweet? Guiltily you clear the palate with
the good bread accompanied by a crock of garlic butter. The suspense
is over, the sweetbreads are here, along with the wine, and Marcel is
vindicated. An exquisite dish as interesting for its textures as its
taste. The sweetbreads loll around with capers, green olives and

button mushrooms all bound together in a cream sauce that's spiked with both brandy and sherry. All the vegetables this evening have been cooked *al dente*, a remarkable feat anytime but a miracle on a Saturday night.

Tarte maison while not in the same league as the rest of the dinner is still very good apple tart. The espresso is splendid.

The next day you learn, casually, that the chef is about to depart, something all chefs everywhere are about to do. The rumor is denied, as rumors always are, but proceed cautiously. Jean Dubuc, formerly of Barbetta in Washington, D.C., would be a hard act to follow.

> L'Hermitage, *Rte. 45, Warren, Conn. 06754. About 5 mi. N of New Preston via Rte. 45. Marcel Rodriguez, Prop. L – noon-2, D – 6-9, till 10 Sat., 1-8 Sun. Closed Mon. and month of Feb. AE, BA, MC. Reservations may be necessary weekends: 203-868-2355.*

Colonial LITCHFIELD is a town rather used to being admired; few lovelier village greens exist in America. THE FIRST CONGREGATIONAL CHURCH is one obvious reason. The very symbol of the New England conscience, it is in fact a faithful rendering in wood of London's St. Mary's-in-the-Fields, recreated (with love) by the lonely émigres. Litchfield is a "found" Williamsburg, the heart of it protected by The National Register as a National Historical District, but a place where life goes on uninterruptedly down the generations.

The countryside is calendar Connecticut: rolling hills, stony pastures, runny brooks, lakes*, steeples – and antique stores (Route 7 is referred to sometimes as Antiques Alley). But it is admittedly too much to bite off for a day trip. Plan to stay at least one night, if you can't make it longer, at

---

KILVAROOK INN
Litchfield, Connecticut

A VERY SEDUCTIVE PLACE, Kilvarook (properly *Kil-rook* but oftener, *Kil-va-rock* – take your choice). Life here is not unlike shipboard, but a ship with 146 acres, four tennis courts, a swimming pool and a billiard table (one each), ski-touring and snowshoeing on 25 miles of adjoining trails; some guests never get as far as Litchfield which is two or three miles further on.

*There are three nearby: Mt. Tom Pond, Bantam Lake, and Lake Waramaug.

Agatha Christie fans will have no trouble recognizing it. There's the sign at the gatepost and under it the name "Phil Hoyt, permittee." Then a long curving drive and at the end an English Tudor house with mullioned windows (yes, they do seem to stare) and a portico'd entrance. The grounds throng with great old well-behaved trees that seem to follow the rich wherever they live, with wilder woods lying in wait far in the back, beyond the topiary garden. Where would a Christie mystery be without its topiary garden?

Inside the stage is set. A fire is burning in the great hall, vast sofas and deep seats are set about on the Oriental rugs. A trickle of people filtering through French doors . . . a few more sipping Scotch and aperitifs on benches near the fire. Abortive efforts on the piano from the direction of the library. *Déjà vu*, mystery readers?

On the library table magazines line up obediently: *Yachting, Business Week*, several *New Yorkers*, one copy of *Ms.*—and *Gourmet*. "My favorite reading," says Liz Hoyt. "I eat up every word in it." An accomplished cook, she has been giving cooking demonstrations and lectures for several years, particularly in the intricacies of the smorgasbord, which, being Danish, she learned at an early age. That's her Danish roast duck on the menu, but for the most part she has turned the kitchen duties over to a past-mistress of pasta and other North Italian specialties. The manicotti which is entirely homemade reaches greatness in these hands, cream on cream, cheese on cheese, not even faintly rouged with tomato, and what pasta! Frog's legs *Provençale* are fully realized too, aswirl with herbs and garlic. The Kilvarook kitchen is known to be well out of the ordinary. On occasion that is very faint praise. Accompaniments are fresh zucchini, potatoes *maison* and an expert salad. There are homemade soups and pleasant but busy-day desserts. The dining room though formal is rather relaxed with no pressure to eat and be gone.

Colonnaded stairs wind up under a leaded glass skylight with rooms opening off it in all directions. The least of them are very comfortable, indeed, and one or two fairly luxurious. The house is heavy with atmosphere . . . it's not at all difficult to understand that one young man who grew up under these high ceilings went on to become head of the Smithsonian. For something lighter, more summery, there's contemporary digs hidden away on the grounds complete with fireplace and living quarters and a kitchenette, fine for families or a reunion of old friends.

Everything's here you could want except a shooting script.

Kilvarook Inn, *Brush Hill Rd., Litchfield, Conn. 06759. Located 2 mi. W of town off Rte. 25. Greyhound bus service out of N.Y. Port Authority Terminal daily. Lis & Phillips Hoyt, Jr., Prop. Open all year for* lodgings. *Dining room closed Wed. and Nov.-Dec. 28 (breakfast will be served inn guests). L – noon-2, till 3 Sat., D – 6-8.30, till 9 Sun. MC only. Reservations essential: 203-567-8100.*

III.

NORTHEAST JERSEY—
THE NEAR COUNTRY

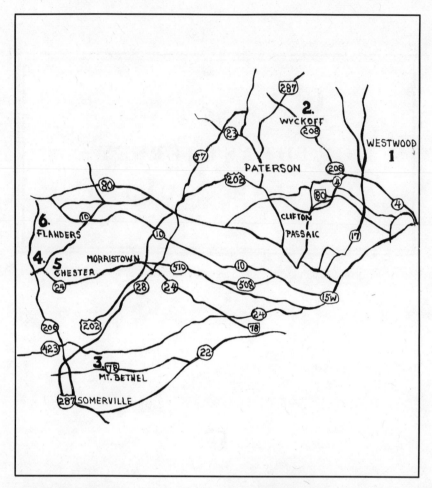

1. FIN 'N' CLAW
2. CERVINO'S BRICK HOUSE
   INN
3. KING GEORGE INN

4. CHESTER INN
5. AUBERGE PROVENCALE
6. SILVER SPRINGS FARM

Public transit companies serving the area: Bus from N.Y.C.—Transport of New Jersey (Westwood); Train from N.Y.C.—Erie-Lackawanna (Basking Ridge, Westwood, Morristown), Central of New Jersey (Somerville).

BEHIND THE

PALISADES

No, THEY HAVEN'T SUCCEEDED in paving over Northeast Jersey at this writing in spite of the awesome population figures. Maybe Union and Hudson, much of Essex. Not all of Passaic County. Not yet Bergen. But the colonization process that began with the Dutch, then the English, etcetera, etcetera, goes on, even now, with all the tribes except the Indians increasing exponentially.

Charming, history-laden Dutch stone dwellings are all around, popping out of the shrubbery almost as frequently as shopping centers. A twist and a turn away from major commercial arteries and deserts like Route 46 you can come upon still-green and charming old towns such as LEONIA. In the lovely town of TENAFLY, the elusive suburban dream is still being sought where suffragist Elizabeth Cady Stanton once lived in a pillared mansion and carried on the struggle to free women from their dollhouses. The incomparable PALISADES have not been toppled yet (though real estate interests are pushing hard) and the HENRY HUDSON DRIVE has more beautiful footage than any fifty-mile stretch anywhere in the East though the porpoises and the sloops and the steamboats have been banished along with the fabled oyster beds and the innocence. At any of several points you can stop-off to record the most admired span in the Western hemisphere and New York's ever-beautiful profile. Or take to the footpaths and explore the Palisades close-up. How lovely to escape from the tyranny of the motorcar where the world passes in front of your eye—but always under glass—and the driver risks life everytime (s)he admires a moving target of a view.

33

Since the restaurants in this part of the state are only a bridge span away from New York's legendary establishments they have to try harder, a loyal resident explains. You'll find some amazingly good kitchens on this side of the river serving a knowledgeable clientele that was weaned on La Côte Basque, La Grenouille, Lafayette and the like. For make no mistake about it, a good restaurant is a tango between the kitchen and the clientele; you can't have one without the other. In addition, now and then, some well-known eating establishment will pack up its pots and pans and emigrate here from the city, like,

---

FIN 'N' CLAW

Westwood, New Jersey

WHAT IS A fastidious and elegant seafood restaurant doing out here in the Bergen boondocks miles from the sea? Miles from even the nearest Hudson shad? It's doing beautifully.

For fifteen years this comfortable old farmhouse-turned-restaurant has been dedicated to the apotheosis of fish and seafood, and customers have been queuing up to jump into the net. Eventually Fin 'n' Claw has had to make room for success, pushing out here, tacking on there. In the process the farm got swallowed up like an unsuspecting oyster, leaving only a bit of hard shell clinging like any mollusk to the svelte new digs. Inside, instead of grinning lobsters and nets stuck with debris of the sea, white linens and silver and space. Recently, the Fin 'n' Claw has acquired a new and distinguished owner, Jacques Jaffrey, a French classicist of a chef himself, who has served as food editor and cooking instructor of *American Home*. But an anonymous Great Man in the kitchen carries on unmolested in his own largely self-taught fashion and teaches the teacher.

It's easy to guess from the crabcakes that the chef comes from the South, the Bayou country actually, where crab is known and understood. The thick-looking crust is not thick at all, just remarkably crunchy and brown. The meat is sweet and lumpy with a minimum of binder and the seasoning is sexier than usual—away with the tartar sauce. Steamed red snapper with lobster sauce is delicate as soufflé, delightful. The meal was launched with a beautiful Boston fish chowder, a *pousse café* of fish flavors. The French fries are not skippable, not this time. The salad is superb, well-dressed greens with a shaving of is it shallot? on top. A large rolling cart of desserts cruises around the room bearing luscious-looking white-capped pies laden with guilt. At this point, M. Jaffrey is beginning to put an oar in, like his chocolate mousse, with more to come. Lunch for two launched with a drink apiece is under $10.00. Dinner will run half again as much. Not that we're complaining. Where else will you find 33 listings under chef's specialties in addition to the many à la carte items? Specialties like *bouillabaisse*, like sauteed abalone "southern seas," like a Bombay seafood curry, like lemon sole *Agraini* (described as a grape sauce)? What price vegetables cooked to order? Ye gods and little fishes, a restaurant that takes the trouble to distinguish between the coarse "deep sea scallops" and the tender little cashew-flavored ones (a dollar more) that are scooped out of a bay is worth its weight in sturgeon.

> Fin & Claw, *644 Pascack Rd., P. O. Westwood, Washington Township, N.J. 07675. (Exit 168 off Garden State Pkwy. and turn rt.) Jacques Jaffrey, Prop. L – noon-3; D – 5-10; noon-8.30 Sun. Closed Mon., Thanksgiving, Christmas. AE, BA, DC, MC, CB. Reservations imperative weekends. 201-664-6141.*

In Northeast New Jersey there are several old inns where the sweet smell of success has not obliterated all the effluvia of the past. The delicate art of feeding lots of people while preserving a sense of intimacy has been learned inside out at

CERVINO'S BRICK HOUSE INN

Wyckoff, New Jersey

THE PINK BRICK inn itself, built in the late 1700's has been neatened and scrubbed till it looks painfully new, but inside, at least in the small tucked-away dining rooms where candlelight throws up a crazy dance of shadows on walls and ceiling, the illusion of another, long-ago time clings. Upstairs among the rafters where old loveseats and sofas and wing-backed chairs meet around coffee tables, the Brick House version of a cocktail lounge, the illusion's even stronger. The wine cellar, advertised as one of the most complete in the East, is upstairs, too—in the **attic**.

Food is prepared with skill, if not inspiration, and served with flair. Be fearless about ordering fish: it's boned for you, expertly, at tableside. Wine rests in ice in stands. Though the self-styled "Continental cuisine" referred to is the *Italian* continent there is little hint overall of the hot breath of a red tomato, let alone a garlic cube. And though you'll meet a stuffed eggplant *Parmigiana* and a *fettucini Caruso* among the dinner specialties and a *fettucini* with peas and prosciutto, even a *canneloni*, on the lunch menu, the standard restaurant items— the steaks, the chops, the duckling—dominate.

Desserts are largely poured out of brandy and cordial bottles (an ice cream *Sombrero* is an Alexander à la mode with pecans), but you can have pecan pie or cheese cake if you like, even an occasional cannoli.

Like so many places with rather steep prices, lunch is a buy. Try it some day en route to or from the BERGEN COUNTY WILDLIFE CENTER. A hamburger with lettuce and tomatoes and French fries is $1.35*, while chopped filet mignon on the table d'hote lunch is $1.95*. (Let McDonald's chew on **that**.)

Cervino's Brick House Inn, *179 Godwin Ave., Wyckoff, N.J. 07481. (Russell Ave. exit off Rte. 208 and go 1 mi.) Michael A. Cervino, Prop. L—11-5, D—5-12 Tues.-Fri., 5-2 Sat., noon-11 Sun. Closed Mon., first 2 wks. of Feb. & July. AE, BA, MC. Reservations a must weekends: 201-891-1929.*

IN THE HUNT
COUNTRY

IN THE MIDDLE of North Jersey you'll find good hunting – antiques, horses, fashion, millionnaires. The heart of it lies between Morristown and Chester, south of Route 24 and north of the Watchungs or Interstate 78, with the best addresses (and the best driving) concentrated south of Mendham. There are exceptions . . . everything won't fit tidily in this box. Oldwick, for instance, over the line on the west for antiques . . . Millburn, the lazy woman's Fifth Avenue, on the east. For millionnaires, look around Peapack, Gladstone, Basking Ridge, Bernardsville, Far Hills, Liberty Corners – the right side of the Erie-Lackawanna tracks which until relatively recently took them into the city each day in their own private, plush car.

Antiques are a light industry hereabouts. They overflow the town of Mendham. For sheer quantity and variety though there's nothing to compare with ARCHIE AND EMMY STILE'S PLACE in Meyersville where the loot from the past covers three acres. For a different sort of hunting expedition the most fabulous place in all Morris County is a prehistoric lake bottom south of Morristown – the GREAT SWAMP NATIONAL WILDLIFE REFUGE. Real estate worth millions of dollars has been reserved for woodchucks and chipmunks, beavers and shrews and voles and moles and mink and mice and deer and 207 species of birds. The observation center, which is off Long Hill Road, has a mile or more of boardwalk and a blind in which the visitor may take refuge. When you come, wear old covering clothes, old boots or sneakers and bring mosquito repellent. The best viewing times are early in the day or late, but never on a Sunday afternoon – nobody's here then but us people.

The best time to view DUKE'S GARDENS* located on Route 206 just below Somerville, is at the end of endless winter. Come under leaden skies in a sleet storm if you can arrange it, over old dirty snow deposits and enter a world where flowers bloom, and plants obey, and nature makes a spectacle of herself. Grottoes, jungles, Edwardian conservatories, gardens like nosegays from the past . . . eleven settings from different times and places under an acre of glass.

For a hint of the way it was at JOCKEY HOLLOW in 1779-80, don't come in the spring. Jockey Hollow is a picnic in the spring, a forest preserve laced with wildflower trails. No, come in deepest winter when ponds are frozen fast and the ground rings like rock. When the Continental Army camped in this spot three miles south of Morris-

*One-hour tours by appointment only. Admission, $1.75.

town, the snow reached four feet high in places and the dead were buried in it like so many sheep. That winter which saw 28 snowfalls, and saw the Hudson and the Delaware freeze over from shore to shore, is said to have been more murderous than the winter of Valley Forge. The troops, miserably fed, lived and slept in nothing more than tents, and some, according to an eye-witness, went about "naked as Lazurus." The FORD MANSION, Washington's headquarters in Morristown, and the nearby HISTORICAL MUSEUM is said to have the most important collection of Washington memorabilia north of Mt. Vernon . . . and it's nice and warm. Start there.

The story goes that when certain citizens of Mt. Bethel complained to the tavernkeeper of the drinking and rowdiness overflowing onto the streets and the very doorsteps of the church, he pointed out, reasonably enough, that the tavern was there first. Subsequently, when a law was passed requiring such establishments to keep a respectful distance from a house of worship, he erected a fence that routed the customers through a kind of maze, thus negotiating the required legal distance before entering. We don't know what moral there is in the fact that the church has moved on down the road while the former Mt. Bethel Inn remains, known to a happy constituency as

KING GEORGE INN
Mt. Bethel, New Jersey

THE INN is high in the Somerset Hills, overlooking a wide, satisfactory sweep of countryside, across the street from an old cemetery.

Miles away there's a slow coil of smoke, one "poetic curl of pollution," according to a spectator. No wonder that early innkeeper clung to his ground – he didn't want to give up the view.

If you feel the same way, ask to eat upstairs in the new Crow's Nest, but if you want to dine where those early patrons put it away, hug the hearths downstairs, especially in the taproom. Notice, please, the bark still clinging to the old low beams overhead. This part is said to go back to 1692 and was once a blacksmith shop. There's Whitbread's English beer available if you'd like to drink to that.

When it comes to restorations Dorothy Hayden is something of a gourmet herself: everything in the place reflects her passion for authenticity – tables, chairs, the many collector's items. Even the flowers.

In the kitchen Maximillian Hayden, a man who can stand the heat and stood it for some forty years, can still be found, supported by a large cast of Haydens and old-faithfuls. He's supervising now, and one son is a chef. The same intolerance of imitation prevails here. Raw materials are the best available, especially the meats, and much of the butchering is done on the premises. Soups are good home brews, vegetables like the creamed spinach generally fresh, mashed potatoes earthy and not poured out of a cardboard box. Fried oysters in their jackets of brown crumbs are juicy inside . . . so are the pork chops, grilled-to-order and generous in size. Little hot biscuits are homemade, but the apple strudel which is à la carte runs a poor second to the homely rice pudding that comes with the lunch, rice pudding that's both meltingly creamy and *al dente* and never too sweet.

Lunch is a serious meal at King George; but you can have a proper sandwich if that's what you want. For the highly regarded *sauerbraten* with *kartoffle klosse*, the steamed King crab, the broiled duckling, you must come dinnertime or Sunday afternoon – and bring the family.

> King George Inn, *181 Mt. Bethel Rd., Warren, N.J. 07060. Located on a hilltop 4½ mi. off Rte. 22 (take Warrenville Rd. N 4½ mi.). M. James Hayden, Prop. L – noon-2 Tues.-Sat.; D – 5.30-9 Tues.-Fri.; 5-10 Sat., noon-7 Sun. Closed Mon. and during last wk. of July & first 2 wks. Aug. AE, MC. Sat. reservations a must: 201-647-0410.*

There's one talented chef on the eastern seaboard who won't be throwing the *doboschtorte* at the boss and walking out the night before you get there. He's Rolf Eiring, a German wunderkind who at age twenty-two ran the Löwenbräu Gardens at the New York World's Fair. He and the suave Egon Groman, a former chief steward on the Hamburg Line, went into partnership and bought a beautiful old wreck called the

CHESTER INN

Chester, New Jersey

ROOM BY ROOM BY ROOM (there are 50!), they have proceeded to salvage this once-elegant old place, built in 1812, a former stage stop and refueling station for settlers moving west in covered wagons. The white brick facade with its commanding pillars still confronts the motorized world like a well-mannered rebuke. It's not surprising to find a Mr. Pullman's name inscribed in the 1890's register, a proud trophy that's kept under the bar. The inn has been many things to many people over the years.

If you come on a Friday or Saturday night, you'll be greeted by a muffled explosion of Dixieland back in the ballroom. This honorable American folk art has been installed here for years where the new owners are keeping it warm for the time when the world is safe for good hot jazz again.

The other Chester Inn tradition being revived is superb food.

All the entrées are prepared while you wait and to wait with there's well-iced relishes, the olives bigger than the pictures on the cans, and a dense heavy-crusted German white bread still breathing steam under napkin cradle. Then a small triumph of a Caesar salad with tiny *homemade* buttered croutons; it's presented without the live, right-before-the-eyes performance which turns out to be unnecessary after all. Set up for the kill, it comes at last: true beef *Stroganoff*. The fingers of steak are still rosy-rare in the middle, and in the subtle seductive sauce you discover transparent shavings of cornichons, a delicious note. A mix of wild and white rice is served with it, and cauliflower which could be crisper if you may carp at a restaurant that has served you so well.

"People come here from all over," Egon Gruner sighed sadly, "telling me they've heard about our food . . . then they order steak." He shrugs. The menu is unstartling, conventional, until you come to the chef's specials – stuffed filet of flounder with lobster *a l'Americaine* . . . venison, hunter style . . . steak-and-oysters in Burgundy . . . an elegant boneless stuffed duckling in port wine and wildest of all, veal steak with asparagus and King crabmeat in a white wine sauce, a superb, if improbable, dish.

There's strawberries Romanoff for dessert, a coupe of fresh, perfumed strawberries dragged across the snows of winter and blanketed in Grand Marnier sauce, or the chef's own light, lovely Black Forest torte.

The Chester Inn is in good hands, all right. The chef's, the chief steward's, and the bartender's, too. Together they are plastering, painting, snatching curlicued brass-and-iron beds from oblivion and setting them glowing again, muffling the graceful stairs and the groaning old halls in carpeting. Yes, they should be ready for you by the time you get there, and yes, the chef will be back in the kitchen.

> Chester Inn, *111 Main St., Chester, N.J. 07930. Rolf Eiring & Egon Gronau, Prop. L – 11.30-2.30, D – 5.30-9.30, till 10.30 Fri., till 11 Sat., Sun. 1-8.30. Closed Tues.* Lodgings. *AE, BA, MC. Phone: 201-879-7574.*

Fate is running true to form. Once in France after a six-hour chase this reporter arrived too late to eat at the famed Fernande Point's Restaurant de la Pyramine. Now, three years after chef-owner Pierre Bellager has moved to Florida, we have come to

---

AUBERGE PROVENÇALE
Chester, New Jersey

THIS LITTLE HOUSE lit year-round with a string of red-yellow-blue-green Christmas tree lights is a famous place, perhaps the most famous restaurant in all New Jersey. The restaurant along with its reputation has been handed over to eager disciples, but not just **any** disciples. The present chef, who with his tall athletic hulk and straggly blond hair seems to have wandered in the kitchen by mistake, said in awe, in disbelief even: "It took me two months of apprenticeship under M. Bellager before I mastered everything on the menu." This, after serving as a chef in the army!

It is quite a menu to master in two months. *Bouillabaisse*, a Friday night specialty, is listed modestly enough as fish soup *Marseillaise*. Unfortunately, the modesty is earned for the soup is a bit timid, while the duck pâté makes up for it and comes on too strong. But the pheasant *maison** is a pure pleasure, and is presented whole in its casserole with a flourish of tailfeathers before being whisked away for "saucing" and serving. Puréed chestnuts help even more. The *coquilles St. Jacques* come off very well too, nuttily sweet in a sauce of pure velvet. Peas *à la français* and rice *Milanaise* offer fine support, but those oversoft Belgian canned carrots ought to be banned before they give carrots a bad name. At this visit desserts are still being "worked out." The French pasteries are the product of two nearby bakeries of uneven merit, but there's quite good selection of vintage cheeses as comfort.

Since Auberge Provencale has no liquor license you are encouraged to bring your own wine, a factor that lightens the tab considerably, making dinner here little more than dinner elsewhere. Perhaps this is what brings out your tolerance. Or perhaps it's the way the waitresses scurry for you and worry over you. What if the fruit on the buffet table turns out to be wax? What if bread is Jewish rye, and Napoleons are *Italian* napoleons (wasn't Napoleon himself half-Italian?) If you like lotteries, it is possible to eat well here. There is a spirit on these premises that asks to be respected. Well-meaning men have taken it on themselves to provide an alternative to prime ribs and baked potato sloshed with sour cream. Bumbling Americans are attempting to conquer the mysteries of *la haute cuisine*, taking a gamble on greatness. If they are still in business when you call for your reservation, it would be safe to say they have succeeded.

> Auberge Provencale, *Main St. (Rte. 24), Chester, N.J. 07930. Jos. F. Scrudato, Prop. L (summers only) — 11.30-2; D — 6.30-9 Tues.-Thurs., till 9.30 Fri. & Sat., 3.30-8 Sun. Closed Mon., vacation. Sat. reservations essential: 201-879-5421.*

Not infrequently the *haute-est cuisine* is found in unlikely settings. One of the most celebrated kitchens in France, *Les Frères Troisgrois*, huddles down by the railroad tracks in the small, unloveable, even ugly town of Roanne. In New Jersey, now, the most ambitious French cuisine is served in an echo chamber with linoleum floors, in a room so brightly lit the conventional rustic candle in the wine jug is powerless against it. *Voilà*, the

*Must be ordered in advance.

SILVER SPRINGS FARM
Flanders, New Jersey

NOTHING IS *comme il faut* at Silver Springs. No maitre d', no self-important florist's flowers, no press of tables, no flotilla of wine glasses, a wine list that neglects to cite year, and lists only one Bordeaux. Instead, there are rules and regulations, as in school, as in camp. Reservations must be made well in advance, a minimum of four to a party on Fridays and six on Saturdays. Dinner is ordered days or even weeks ahead from an elaborate menu which is mailed to your home. Most difficult of all, everyone in a party must eat the same thing. The chances of finding four or six people who can agree on *mousse de poisson sauce Nantua* over *quenelle sauce Aurore* without harboring secret resentment is slimmer than the odds on finding fresh truffles in Central Park. No, nothing is *comme il faut* except the food itself. Undiluted Escoffier.

Hors d'oeuvres are on the house, a great platter of very hot stuffed clams, mussels, escargots, and fried shrimp. The waitress insists every last morsel be consumed. ("What! You're leaving *this*?" pointing to the failed fried shrimp) before bringing on a beautiful *billi-bi* which tastes like cream-of-sea. We are invited to admire the fish mousse, then to partake. Your luck is holding. But, it's the *Chateaubriand*, rare, utterly tender, with *bordelaise* sauce that persuades you of your wisdom in coming. Plump little souffled potato puffs accompany this and broccoli hollandaise.

Yes, it's true, butter is plunked down just as it comes out of the wrapper, and the cheeses, when offered, are fresh out of the refrigerator, chilled to the marrow. (Remove a star.) *Crêpes soufflés* with custard sauce come along just in time. (Put it back.) The courtesy platter of cookies arrives two bars after the finale. (Stare in stupor.)

In summer the farmhouse with its barn-like sleeping quarters looks like some sort of camp. It **is** a sort of camp, largely patronized by French expatriates, often refugees themselves from the restaurant business as well as from the city. They stick a sign in the window– "Closed"–just as in Paris during the *fermeture annuelle*–and go to the country with their families to walk, to swim, to pick berries, to play soccer or tennis or bocce, to luxuriate in the one, the pure-and-only mother tongue and to eat some good home cooking. For in summer, Silver Springs Farm also serves a simple potluck dinner ($6 per person) which might include something like a fish mousse or a tureen of *bouillabaisse* to start, then a juicy roast ham or home-made sausages with puréed peas, succotash, salad. For dessert, a *crème caramel*. (Home is not Topeka, Kansas.)

Perish sauce *Périgourdine*. A pox on your *veau Cordon Bleu*. To the bottom of the sea with *homards Américaine* & *Thermidor*. And please pass the bread so we can mop up the ham drippings.

> Silver Springs Farm, *Drakestown Rd., Flanders, N.J. 07836. Located 5 mi. N of Chester off Rte. 206. The Ivaldi family, Prop. Haute-cuisine Fri. & Sat., also weeknights and Sun. for large parties; family dinners (no choice, but call the morning before for menu) on Sun. (1 pm) and during summer. Summer lodgings with breakfasts available. Reservations must be made in advance: 201-584-6660.*

IV.
MONMOUTH COUNTY— SURF 'N' TURF

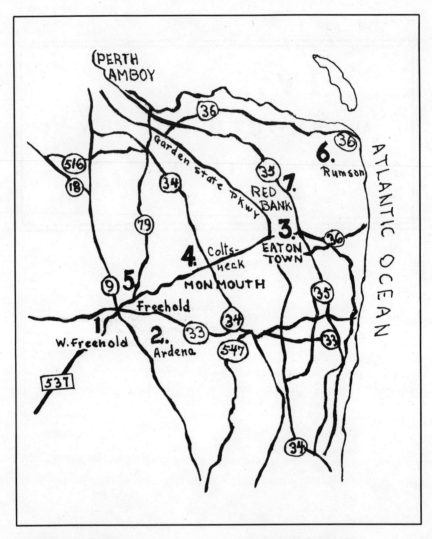

1. **MOORE'S INN**
2. **OUR HOUSE TAVERN**
3. **OLD ORCHARD INN**
4. **DELICIOUS ORCHARDS**
5. **AMERICAN HOTEL**
6. **RUMSON HOTEL**
7. **MOLLY PITCHER INN**

Public transit companies serving the area: Bus from N.Y.C.—Transport of New Jersey (Freehold, Eatontown, Red Bank), Lincoln Transit (Freehold), Asbury Park-New York Transit (Eatontown, Red Bank); Bus from Phila.—Transport of New Jersey (Freehold); Train from N.Y.C.—New York and Long Branch (Red Bank).

IT MAY HAVE BEEN the heat, extraordinary by all reports, that actually won the disputed Battle of Monmouth on the plains of East Jersey in June 1778, but the British got the message—the "rabble" meant business. The BATTLEFIELD, which is near FREEHOLD, is a park now, marked by both a plaque and a well that pays tribute to the courage of our first woman soldier; Molly "Pitcher," or Molly Ludwig Hays, was inscribed as a sergeant in the official Army roster by General Washington for taking up her husband's post by the cannon when he fell wounded. Cemetery browsers should look up OLD TENNANT CHURCH too, where the wounded were taken and cared for.

If the day is Saturday, point for ENGLISHTOWN and its FLEAMARKET which people in this area attend more regularly than church. An archeologist might reconstruct the past fifty to a hundred years of life in America from the debris spread out on these acres. For the best hunting, some before dawn's early light when the stallkeepers are first setting out their wares—and bring your flashlight like the dealers do. Later, it's still a good show for people-watchers of the world, and you can always buy a latter-day antique like a pressure cooker or bargains like one-legged panty hose. *That* kind of thing.

Freehold is the county seat of Monmouth. Further mementoes of the battle and the past are plentiful, but if you happen to hear the patter of hooves it's not the ghost of Major General Charles Lee retreating with the cavalry. It's the trotters at FREEHOLD RACEWAY or the runners at nearby MONMOUTH PARK. Horseracing is taken very seriously around here. Early settlers—no Puritans—were known to be fond of the sport and raced their horses on King's Highway near Middletown. Organized racing has been going on locally for over a century (with time out for legal considerations).

Near the Freehold track is a funky sort of place, a prehistoric stage coach stop, dear to the hearts of harness racers and local gentry. They haven't changed a *thing* in a hundred years, we're told, at

---

MOORE'S TAVERN

West Freehold, New Jersey

... EXCEPT the old pot-bellied stove the regulars used to sit around cracker-barrel style. It's gone now, replaced by a TV set. At certain hours the din's so great it's impossible to pick up tips anymore, as in the good gone days, by eavesdropping, or to get a drink without shouting. Yet, there's a true country flavor to the place, beginning with the host and barkeep Jim Carney on down to the rocking chairs and the peanut shells on the floor. An inventory of all the signs, notices, bric-a-brac, pictures and packaged snacks that cover the walls and of the bodies looped over the tables and bar would take days.

By moving on to the adjoining Turkey Swamp Room it's possible to escape the bulldozing bleat of the TV (but not guaranteed: an auxiliary set awaits a turn of the screw). This is relative grandeur, sitting at a table, in a room full of holy relics of the track. A prized collection of racing silks, or driver's colors as they're called in harness racing, once worn by the greats, surround you. They droop now on their thin wire hangers from wherever someone happened on a nail in the wall as though waiting to be claimed at the end of a losing race, but keep you from feeling alone, to say the least.

Here you may sit till you rot with never a drop to eat.

> Moore's Tavern, *RD 3, West Freehold, N.J. 07728. Located 1 mi. W of Freehold on Rte. 537. Jim Carney, Prop. Open 8 am-2 am Mon.-Sat., 12-12, (usually) Sun., 8 am-noon and Thanksgiving Day. Closed Christmas. Phone: 201-363-6811.*

For food you have to go elsewhere, perhaps to what is fondly referred to as Turkey Swamp* Room East or,

OUR HOUSE TAVERN
Ardena, New Jersey

THE SIGN is startlingly simple, "Chicken . . . Turkey Dinners" it reads, and there is the old tavern tucked into a bend of the road be-

---

*Turkey Swamp is the name of a nearby park.

hind a shroud of shrubbery and a long narrow porch. It was just about here that pine baron Louis Fenton, member of the notorious Fagan gang, got his. The PINE BARRENS which are sneaking up around us now have always been hospitable to cutthroats and thieves and the business of murder and are used even today as a dumping ground for Mafia victims.

Near the entrance a cast-off, cast-iron stove leans up against the house turning orange in the sun. No bodies today.

To get to the dining area you must first go down a hall past a storeroom full of flea-market flotsam and through the kitchen itself where wires are strung overhead in loops, like a clothesline. Has there been a mistake? Have you come by the wrong door? To the wrong place? The chef, Tony Bianchini, is reassuring. "Did you see that old stove outside?" he wants to know. "It's nearly ninety-years-old. This is our new one," indicating it with his head. "This one's just thirty. Took us nearly a whole year to find another coal-burning stove," he says, not without pride. This is the same man, a drop-out from big-time food management services, who told his wife after interviewing for this post: "Would you believe what they're cooking on down there? I haven't even *seen* one since I left the army" . . . that was some years ago and now he pats the new model as another man might a Stutz Bearcat.

If you get the nod, you may be allowed to join the club in the Turkey Swamp Room East where Lucy Beaumont, the owner, is installed behind the bar. This is her turf, where she grew up, and her father before her. Or maybe a table in the "private" room, part of the original house, where there's a fireplace. More likely you'll find yourself in one of the newer rooms, mollified by a view of the countryside.

It's not strictly true that the menu hasn't been altered in the two hundred years Our House Tavern has been in operation, as rumored. Guinea hen — become hard to get — is gone, and the menu is distinctly shorter than it was. More to the point is the innocence of the offerings. Nothing is stuffed with crabmeat. Chicken is not honey-dipped or "dipt." Obviously, they don't speak gourmay here. Food is food and you don't fool around with it. No orange sauce mystique is allowed to distract you from the true flavor of a beautifully fired duck. Take it as it comes, all naked and brown and homely—**and isn't it good!** You can ignore the sauceboat of dark pan gravy (a bit bitter) and the bread and onion stuffing (a bit pasty) and give yourself up to any number of side attractions that are flocking around your plate much as if some doting relative had emptied the larder at the news of your visit. The waitress who has dark tragic eyes and white hair drawn gently back into a knot moves with a touching, rather uncertain grace: does this please you? Does that? She comes and goes with a salver of relishes on ice, a homemade clam chowder that's halfway between Manhattan and New England and not bad, green bean salad, Belgian carrots, cranberries, a mound of pan fries cooked to several crisps with onions and never bettered.

Steaks are seared directly on open coals and the big thing here is the Pittsburgh broil, i.e. steak charred to a crisp on the outside but remaining rare, rather than pink, on the inside. In a world where one chef's "medium rare" is another chef's pot roast, this should help close the communication gap.

Prices are another charming anachronism, and very good for the digestion. Unless you insist on pheasant with wild rice (order ahead ... $9.00 on the dinner) or one of the steaks ($7.75 and $8.75), the average dinner is around $6.00. There are two choices under $5.00, both complete. This day, "complete" includes **fresh** strawberry shortcake whipped up by the chef, good and rather unexpected in the middle of February in the middle of nowhere. There are homemade pies, too, on the menu but these look like the fly-gathering, gloppy pies that have made ice cream America's favorite dessert. Stick with the cake.

> Our House Tavern, *Rte. 524, Ardena, N.J. 07727. Located south of Freehold near Allaire Deserted Village. Lucy Beaumont, Prop. L — noon-2.30; D — 5-8.30 Wed.-Fri., till 9.30 Sat., 1-8.30 Sun. Closed Mon. & Tues. and last 2 wks. in Feb. For parties over 5, reservations needed: 201-938-5159.*

It doesn't happen often that two people agree on a restaurant but when polling in this part of the world your Rumson bon vivant, the woman at the baked goods counter, state trooper — **all** say the best place to eat, if you can afford it, is

OLD ORCHARD INN
Eatontown, New Jersey

REMEMBER THE OLD Newarker at Newark airport where families used to drive from miles around for the sky-watching and the even more spectacular food? The pro responsible for that and other equally successful restaurant enterprises (C.B.S. Ground Floor, L'Étoile, and the revived Rainbow Room and Grill) has taken a stand in this unlikely spot and is providing classy French cuisine for a crowd that has been subsisting on roast beef with sour-cream-plied baked potato or maybe a flash-frozen crabmeat-stuffed filet of sole between jaunts to New York, San Francisco and Paris. Here, in the wilderness, *filet de sole Tout-Paris* (poached in wine with lobster and glacéed with two sauces): *tournedo Rossini* (filet mignon in red wine sauce with goose liver and mushrooms)! *ris de veau hermétique* (calves' sweetbreads in sherry and cream in pastry shells)! It is too much all at once, and perhaps one is inclined to drink it in too gratefully, but the food, taken as a whole, is both ambitious and successful.

Decisions, decisions. The cowardly way out is the assorted hot hors d'oeuvres immortalized by one remarkable crisped shrimp, swollen as a lobster claw, with orange sauce. Then watercress vichyssoise — a lovely unboring vichyssoise revived with watercress, or a large tureen of very good onion soup, thickly gratinéed. A pause is filled with the house salad of well-dressed greens. It might have been better to fill those pauses with a few holes of golf as portions are over-generous and the best is yet to come.

Comes *sole Tout-Paris*, beautifully coiled under its two sauces of pink and cream . . . or comes lobster, coraled by sauce *Joinville*. Both fill already overindulged diners with great happiness. (The guest with the flat undemanding veal *Cordon Bleu* may be better off — ultimately that is.)

Dessert is feast or famine. Famine if you order the chocolate mousse drawn daintily on the plate with a pastry tube to resemble a miniature éclair, and tied with a shoe string of whipped cream. Feast if it's chocolate fondue with its treasury of dipping fruits and cake morsels, or the beautifully put-together *vacherin glacé*.

Dinner with one drink and wine will wind up over $15 but you can pay for it with what you save at **lunch**. Lunch, costs little more than the tariff at your friendly neighborhood diner, and wines too, unusually well chosen, are not inflated in price.

The restaurant itself is a comfortably upholstered country club overlooking a golf course and nothing therein — certainly not the waitresses dressed like a lot of unemployed Rockettes — tip you off to the elegance of the food.

Aside from such minor carping, compliments to the chef-director, Fred Blattner, and staff.

> Old Orchard Inn, *Rte. 71, Eatontown, N.J. 07724. Located just off Rte. 36 between Eatontown and Long Branch. F. K. Platzer, Prop. L — 12.30-3; D — 5.30-10 Mon.-Fri., till 10 Sat., 1-9 Sun. Closed Christmas Day. AE, DC. Phone: 201-542-9300.*

Colt's Neck and environs is where the horse farms are, and a fine old namesake inn which played a small part in the Revolution. (The interior unfortunately is mauled and the kitchen is a muddle.) Right around here was probably the most successful commune that ever existed in America, the NORTH AMERICAN PHALANX, based on the grand design for restructuring society of Charles Fourier, a French-man. For a little while on its 673 acres this group of like-minded people, hungry for Utopia *now*, actually realized such still remote goals as the 30-hour week, equal pay for men and women, job rotation, day care, self-sufficiency. Women of the phalanx went about in a kind of Turkish trouser and scandalized the neighbors. The commune survived the lean years, but was undone by its own success. A fire finished it off. Succeeding fires wiped out the last standing remains. All that lives on of that noble experiment is the institution of the American boxed cereal breakfast which it started.

Around the corner a popular roadside stand is almost single-handedly keeping alive one of the most endangered of American traditions, good old apple pie. Aim for

---

DELICIOUS ORCHARDS
Colt's Neck, New Jersey

ON THESE UNPREPOSSESSING PREMISES there is open-faced or two-crust apple pie so glorious it makes you proud to be an American! There must be half a peck of fresh, bouncy apples in every pie and the rich, crumbly crust is grand, simply grand, right down to the ground. (The decline and fall of apple pie was speeded in recent years by the widespread use of canned apples by bakeries and restaurants alike, an economic boon but a gastronomic disaster. All pie lovers should take it as a patriotic duty to boycott these inferior products and explain clearly why.)

The good matrons of Rumson could not celebrate Thanksgiving without the aid of Delicious Orchards' pumpkin pies. In addition there's homemade bread and cakes and cookies and pie shells. There's cider doughnuts and homemade cider by mug or jug, to wash them down. There are pyramids of uncommon green groceries brought to you in the flower of their youth (look for baby carrots, thumb-sized zucchini, bibb lettuce, chives) even on the bleakest winter days. If you know your apples, you get the pick of them here, but despite their name Delicious Orchards is not notably partisan to the showy, flavor-bankrupt red Delicious beloved by supermarket buyers and fruitbowls. On a Sunday as many as four policemen have been called upon to direct traffic in and out of these premises. Reason enough.

> Delicious Orchards, *Rte. 34, Colt's Neck, N.J. 07722. Located just south of Rte. 537 crossing, about 6 mi. E of Freehold. The Barclay & Smith families, Prop. Open 9-6*

daily, 1-6 Sun. Closed all major holidays/holiday week-
ends. Phone: 201-462-1989.

If you'd like to linger or even malinger in Monmouth there are
three hotels to choose from. The first was built in 1824 and is located
in the county seat, the busy, bustly

AMERICAN HOTEL
Freehold, New Jersey

How CHARMING it looks from the street with its iron lace balcony
planted with real sulkies. Inside, more charm and a veritable museum
of racing memorabilia. Currier and Ives prints line the halls and in the
dining rooms ancestral prints of horse royalty. Stop in for a drink
and a tour, but neither the rooms upstairs nor the food downstairs
live up to this setting. Rooms are motel-neat and clean, nothing
more, and the food merely edible. The chef is in command of too
many battle stations and too few things come out the way they should.
On Friday nights there's a smorgasbord which is becoming a code
word for "steam-table," as in cafeteria, but it's quite popular.

> *American Hotel, E. Main St., Freehold, N.J. 07728. Richard
> Daesner, Prop. Open daily year-round. L – 11.30-3, D –
> 5-10, from noon Sun. Lodgings and bkfst. Phone: 201-
> 462-0819.*

You can smell the sea while rocking away on the porch of

RUMSON HOTEL
Rumson, New Jersey

THIS HOTEL can be considered a local guesthouse for this well-
favored community. Visitors' rooms are booked for them by the month
or the summer. You're welcome to what's left.

The architecture is the anomalous architecture of so many big
sprawling ocean-confronting houses from the near past still found on
the Jersey shore in places like Deal and Mantoloking. Rooms are
furnished with large whiffs of nostalgia (flowered papers . . . painted
iron bedsteads . . . footed bathtubs . . . maybe a balcony planted with
petunias). There's a dining room, too, and a bar. The restaurant down-

stairs operates year round offering undistinguished food in a pink and pretty dining room overlooking a garden.

> The Rumson Hotel, *10 Waterman Ave., Rumson, N.J. 07760. Near ocean. Open daily year-round. D−6-10, till midnight Sat. Brunch 12-3 Sun.* Lodgings. *AE. Phone:* 201-842-2000.

Then there's the

MOLLY PITCHER INN
Red Bank, New Jersey

A SMALL, well-run hotel is what it is, and harder to find than rubies in the streets. In a world where such places are going to seed faster than they can build Holiday Inns, the high-school-Federal Molly Pitcher, only a half-century old, might be considered for a national historical landmark in another dozen years. Since the Twenties when it was built, it has been the "nice" place to take the family for a Sunday dinner. If the food was neglible, the view was and is splendid. It splashes itself across the entire far wall of the dining rooms, the wide-flung, luminous Navasink River basin. In deep winter, slashed with ice boats' thrilling passage that can easily reach 90 miles per hour. In summer, choppy with sailboats and yachts and launches. Sundays, if you remember to reserve a table by the window, you can watch the races and have your cake too, or sip a hot toddy at the bar while wind-chased ice boats skitter and scud across the frozen surface. *Soft!*

Now, in addition, there is a better-than-average chef, Hans Zbinden, taking over the helm—Swiss, former resident chef of the New York's Tavern-on-the-Green. He knows what he's doing and what he's doing isn't bad. In addition to the touchstones of continental hotel cuisine, the consommés, the entrecôtes, you might encounter something Swissier like a *Bundner Teller* (a platter of typically Swiss dried meats) and welcome it is. He also likes to take shrimp or frog's legs or, by some legerdemain, a whole but *boned* trout, dip it in an ale batter and deep fry. The crust is almost frothy and at the same time exquisitely crisp, and you don't really need the accompanying sweet-sour sauce or the waterlogged potatoes *du jour* (*boulanger* this *jour*). Weeknights in the fall of the year game is offered, including such unusual fare as mouflon (wild sheep) and Canadian elk. All baking is done on the premises but the chef is noted for his chocolate mousse. Deservedly.

The lobby is neo-Williamsburg interspersed with collections of old plates and pewter (the dining room displays include rows of Toby jugs and a stock of muskets). The spit and polish is dazzling. No spiders could feel cozy in such an environment and despite the years there's not a trace of a shadow of life-scar. Lucky hotel — the owner is said to be a millionaire who runs this place for the fun of it, for the like of himself and his friends. And they come, pulling their yachts behind and tying them up in the backyard, some for the whole summer.

Rooms, as you would expect, do not lack for comfort, particularly the corner rooms which are more like living than sleeping quarters. There's an attached motel for those who want to jump from bed to boat without ringing for an elevator.

Molly Pitcher Inn, *Hwy. 35, Red Bank, N.J. 07701. Located 49 mi. from N.Y. on the banks of the Navesink River. Frank J. Monica, Mgr. L — noon-2.30; D — 6-9.30 Mon.-Sat., 1-9 Sun. Lodgings. AE, DC, MC. Phone: 201-747-2500.*

V.

ISLAND OF PRINCETON

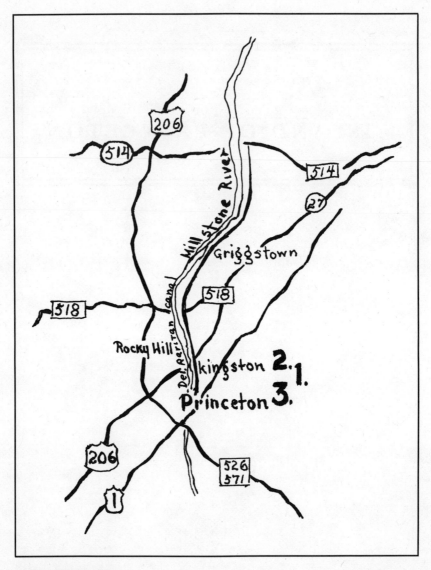

1. **PEACOCK INN**
2. **NASSAU INN**
3. **LAHIÈRE'S**

Public transit companies serving the area: Bus from N.Y.C. – Suburban Transit; Bus from Phila. – Greyhound; Train from N.Y.C. *or* Phila. – Penn-Central (change at Princeton Junction).

THE BATTLE OF TRENTON and the BATTLE OF PRINCETON were psychological turning points of the Revolution. Washington crossed the Delaware more than once, the first time crossing over to the Pennsylvania side with a band of defeated men who had taken a terrible beating. There was no painter then or later to commemorate *this* passage. A short time after, on a desperate gamble, he crossed back and struck a blow against the drunken Hessians in Trenton. In Princeton a few days later, surprised by the British and vice versa, the Americans gave as good as they got. NASSAU HALL passed back and forth three times, it is said, before the Americans withdrew up the back roads to Morristown.

Even if the bumps and ridges and hollows of battlefields and the brilliant plots of generals and reports of troop clashes don't set your mind racing and your pulse thudding . . . even if the children aren't studying Am. Hist. this term, there's another good reason for camp-following these brave men. The loops they made take you through some of the less beaten tracks of New Jersey, through a string of villages that look like a village ought to look and some pretty country not yet tidied up into proper suburban plots.

The first loop from Princeton-to-Washington Crossing links the villages of KINGSTON, ROCKY HILL, HOPEWELL, PENNINGTON, and WASHINGTON CROSSING, a round trip of about 50 miles. (The side trip to TRENTON is recommended only for history buffs.)

The second loop follows two historic waterways—the MILLSTONE RIVER and its satellite, the DELAWARE & RARITAN CANAL that runs alongside. Starting at Princeton where the Millstone has been dammed into a lake, go out Route 27, the former King's Highway, to KINGSTON, making a left in the middle of town onto Route 518. ROCKINGHAM, where Washington wrote and delivered his Farewell Address to the Army is two miles down this road. ROCKY HILL, which is worth investigating, is a little farther (the Reuben's at the ROCKY HILL INN are also worth investigating). Go over the bridge and take the left fork to pick up Canal Road. Funny little backwater towns once clamorous with canal traffic swim by: GRIGGSTOWN, BLACKWELL'S MILLS, MILLSTONE, and WESTON, where the idyll ends. If you're returning to Princeton take the River Road back. Allow three hours in all, more if you like to poke around old churches, grist mills, backsmithys, canal locks, old houses.

The same trip can be accomplished in two days by canoe, tunneling between Kingston and Griggstown in a twilight of old water birches that meet overhead . . . easing by a lotusland of yellow water lilies overflowing the banks of the upper river. Canoes can be rented at Kingston at the little park by the bridge, or in Millstone at the bridge.

Or you could walk along THE TOWPATH, as poetic a byway as there is in the East, or bring a bicycle. Try out the stretch between Kingston and Rocky Hill or Rocky Hill and Griggstown, buoyed in the fall on a blanket of leaves as you go in sweet pursuit of the miles. When the soldiers of the Revolution came this way after giving the British the slip it's unlikely they had time or inclination to admire the country, and the canal and its towpath were not yet built and abandoned.

With a whole weekend to spend in the Princeton area your strategy might be to put up at PEACOCK INN, a popular after-game gathering place for old grads, at 20 Bayard Lane with pleasant rooms and food which though fairly simply prepared is *well*-prepared. Or if you prefer the middle of town there's the NASSAU INN which is centuries younger than it looks, having been built in 1937, but is quite comfortable and just a few yards from historic NASSAU HALL and PRINCETON UNIVERSITY.*

> Peacock Inn, 20 *Bayard Lane (Rte. 206), Princeton, N.J. 08540. Agnes & F. C. Swain, Prop. L — 11-2.30 Mon.-Fri.; D — 5.30-9 Mon.-Sat. Closed Sun. and month of July.* Lodgings. *AE, BA, MC. Phone: 609-924-1707.*

> Nassau Inn, *Palmer Square, Princeton, N.J. 08540. James J. O'Connor, Prop. Open daily year-round. Breakfast 7-10; L — noon-2.30, D — 6-10, all day Sat. & till 8.30 Sun.* Lodgings. *Phone: 609-921-7500.*

*There are excellent maps and guides to the area available through the Princeton Historical Society, the Princeton Chamber of Commerce and Hinkson's Stationers. Also daily guided tours of the University are offered by the Orange Key Guide Service at Stanhope Hall.

Julia Childs claims the best food is found in private homes. Certainly this has been true of Princeton where the dinner party has been raised to an art form . . . so many women of talent and training channeling themselves in this way till the children are safely in Yale and Radcliffe. They often spend two, even three, days in preparation for what a former player calls the "cook-off." Even so the remarkable salad dressing often served at these gatherings, a creamy vinaigrette that's never too sharp or too flat, too thick or too thin, that never separates no matter how long it sits in the refrigerator, is likely to be from the kitchen of

LAHIÈRE'S
Princeton, New Jersey

As LONG as most residents of Princeton can remember, Lahière's has been at this spot, limned in lights like some old theatre marquee. By Princeton standards the three-story stucco'd building with brown shutters, the former Central Hotel, is not very old, maybe a little over a hundred years. Still the greatest jolt to the Princeton image in the past quarter-century was not when they put up the towering faculty apartments down by the lake or the Yamasaki "bike rack" (the Woodrow Wilson School of Public and International Affairs), but when they took down the old red toile cafe curtains at Lahière's and replaced them with a bold new floral. Lahière's has expanded, overflowing into the building next door so guests can wait in comfort in the new white Normandy cave. The original Central Hotel dining room is the one with the bar but there are other rooms, upstairs as well as down, all very appetizing-looking with the crispest of flowers and little shaded lamps that permit you to see what you're eating and whom you're eating it with.

The cooking is French, the menu factual. Food is grillé or sauté or braisé or frit or rôti with few fillings or surprises. But you don't go to Lahière's for surprises. You go there for certainties. Sweetbreads, simply braised and set forth on toast. Standards like frog's legs, *coquilles St. Jacques* or mussels in white wine prepared with considerable skill. Calf's liver thinly sliced and cooked as you like it, rare, medium-rare or well-done. The fish is the freshest, and needs and gets few embellishments; some of Lahière's steadiest customers and severest critics (usually one and the same) agree you can't go wrong with their seafood. Vegetables are cooked at staggered times in small amounts.

For some unaccountable reason Lahière's finest hour is the lunch hour. If you want to find out what visiting celebrity is in town, go then. If you want to be sure the soft shells are sautéed to a nice crisp, go then. The potatoes *Lyonnaise* that come with it are homely and good, vegetables suspiciously like fresh, and the salad in the justly celebrated dressing still has the power to astonish. There are also omelettes—the menu lists seven—and major salads. The desserts are the standards with a better-than-average chocolate *mousse* or *crême caramel* or apple betty. Coffee can be depended on. According to the experts, Lahière's wine cellar is flabbergasting. Two hundred different wines, some 10,000 to 12,000 bottles knowledgeably picked up over the years, temperature-controlled and—how civilized—price-controlled.

The founder, Joseph Christen, courtly, correct, is still a fixture. Trained in Switzerland, he came to Princeton from New York's Ritz Carlton where he was maitre d' on the legendary tenth floor that Toscanini, Mary Garden and Daniel Guggenheim called home. It was his wife, a Lahière, whose own professional education started at age twelve in France, who trained the present chef-in-residence over a quarter century ago.

Son Leon Christen is almost always on hand, hosting, troubleshooting, a hostage to standards. There's still no substitute, it seems, for being there. No way to get around tasting the soup or the sauce before sending it forth. Even the best chef must be permitted occasional battle fatigue, no? The photograph on the wall is Einstein, of course. Yes, he ate here from time to time. So did Robert Oppenheimer, and Thomas Mann, Wigner and von Neumann, William Faulkner, Smythe—who can remember them all?

Lahière's, *11 Witherspoon St., Princeton, N.J. 08540. The Christen family, Prop. L—noon-3; D—5-9.30, till 10.30 Sat., and till 9 Sun. Closed Tues. and first 2 wks. Aug. AE, BA, MC. For reservations: 609-921-2798.*

VI.
IN THE
HUNTERDON HILLS

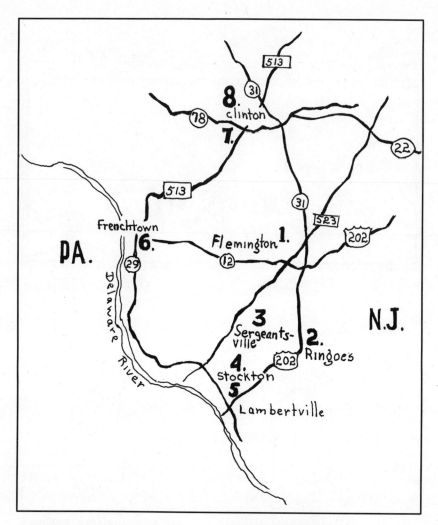

1. UNION HOTEL
2. RINGOES STEAK HOUSE
3. SERGEANSTVILLE INN
4. COLLIGAN'S STOCKTON INN
5. RENAISSANCE
6. FRENCHTOWN NATIONAL HOTEL
7. CLINTON HOUSE
8. BRUNNER'S LANDMARK

Public transit companies serving the area: Bus from N.Y.C.—West Hunterdon Transit (Flemington, Frenchtown, Lambertville), Transport of New Jersey and Martz Trailways (Clinton).

FLEMINGTON

INNS AND OUTS

EVEN ON A DREARY MONDAY at no particular time of the year, the streets of Flemington are clotted with visitors and it's hard to get a table at a restaurant.

What are all these people doing here?

Some have come, doubtless, to pick up seconds of STANGL pottery right at the factory: you can see the kiln across the railroad tracks.* Many more have come to the bazaar called TURNTABLE JUNCTION, a sprawl of thirty or more cottage-shops down by the railroad tracks in a village commons and glutted with objects you may never have known you needed like clan crests and netsukes and do-it-yourself stained glass kits and Christmas decorations in July. To get away from all the commercialism you can move on to LIBERTY VILLAGE,** a somewhat self-conscious eighteenth-century historical recreation where a gunsmith, a candlemaker, a glass-blower, and a blacksmith demonstrate their craft right before the eyes, where Boehm birds and Stiegel glass and other collections are displayed.

Or you can hop a train and ride for over an hour through the undulating landscape between Flemington and Ringoes behind – steam power! Your iron horse, a BLACK RIVER & WESTERN locomotive put to pasture here in the '60's, is a star attraction. Nostalgia-soaked parents and grandparents drag space-age kids to hear that lonesome whistle

---

*Founded in 1805 as Fulper Brothers, making drain tiles.
**Admission: $1.50 adults; $.75 children.

blow, an art form that may someday get the recognition it deserves like weaving or candle-dipping or folk-singing.

At the end of August through Labor Day there's the annual FLEM-INGTON FAIR, a true country brouhaha with ribbon prizes, a fireman's parade and a ferris wheel, stock car races, country and western music, and, in corrals, 4-H lambs as white as snow and pigs pink as poodles. This area has been farming country for two hundred and fifty years, gentlemen farmers now peacefully coexisting with farmer farmers.

But the main thing about this town is the main drag (called fitting-ly enough MAIN STREET), one of the wilder shores of all America, an accidental historical preservation of the nineteenth century. Its collection of Greek Revival houses* and exuberant expressions of Victorian architecture are unmatched anywhere.

Surrounded as you are by restaurants and snack bars, it is easy nonetheless to starve to death in Flemington if you insist on eating **well**, something more substantial, say, than striped cinnamon stick candy or a Texas weiner. True, for emergencies, there's the

---

UNION HOTEL
Flemington, New Jersey

IT'S DIRECTLY ACROSS the street from the HUNTERDON COUNTY COURTHOUSE where the Lindbergh kidnapping trial was held. For 32 days in 1935 this was the center of the world. The hotel itself, built in 1850 and wrapped in a double-decker gallery, resembles a Hollywood set of a carpetbagger hotel to the point of parody. (Where *are* you, Randolph Scott?) The barroom, cleared now of the shoulder-to-shoulder crowd of reporters, has a large, smoothworn bar, a spectacular Italianate mosaic-tiled floor and a mellowness that doesn't come from a bottle.

Take a look at the dining room while you're here. The murals of Indians and Early Settlers and Trees were painted in all innocence in the America of the nineteen twenties. The cooking is what is called "homestyle" if mother never believed in making a fuss over food; the prices are certainly reasonable, and children who hate unfamiliar seasonings, suspicious eaters, will love it. For most of us a look will be enough.

Unfortunately, the Union Hotel is not prepared to accept overnight guests. Bathrooms are few and renovations would be costly, the new

---

*The man behind these facades was a local genius, master-carpenter designer Mahlon Fisher. The Doric House at 116 Main Street was his residence, and is now the home of the Hunterdon County Historical Society.

management reports without noticeable regret. It'll be a while before Victorian architecture is looked upon with the reverence now reserved for Colonial relics and even longer before there's enough money to pay the painters and the plasterers and the plumbers to shore up what's left.

> Union Hotel, *76 Main St., Flemington, N.J. 08822. Ronnie Frostick, Prop. L—11.30-2.30; D—5.30-8 Tues.-Thurs., till 9 Fri. & Sat., 12.30-7 Sun. Closed Mon. evening only, also Christmas & New Year's Day. Phone: 201-782-4311.*

No, take the car and flee. If the kids are hungry, bribe them with ice-cream or the ephemeral waffle cookies from the HUNTERDON EXCHANGE at 155 Main Street. This store, run for the benefit of the Hunterdon Medical Center also has elderly objects and antiques that are quite mildly priced and two or three choice baked goods in the back room. If it's not too late for lunch, take Route 202 (31) to Ringoes. Bear right at the traffic light and in another 400 yards you will see a handsome old fieldstone house on the right with the legend "Amwell Academy . . . 1811" over the doorway. You've come to

---

RINGOES STEAK HOUSE
Ringoes, New Jersey

THE NAME is something of a misnomer. The Yorkes, who have been here over ten years, still dream wistfully of changing the name to the Old Yorke Inn but unfortunately there is an Old Yorke Inn not so very far away. So Ringoes Steak House it remains and you can **have** steak, if you insist, but your host, a former chemist and ex-amateur cook, will be disappointed. He likes tougher assignments *pour le sport*. For dinner, *coq au vin* or *weiner schnitzel* or sweetbreads vermouth (the bill of fare changes from week to week). Give him twenty-four hours notice and four or more willing eaters and he'll throw together an *arroz con pollo* or produce a rack of lamb. If the moon is in the right quarter you may even find Maine lobster on the menu. At lunchtime, however, there is his unheralded masterpiece, the *ultimate* Reuben. (This sandwich, unknown just a few years back when it won a national sandwich contest, may soon sweep even the cheeseburger into oblivion; it appears on virtually every lunch menu in this part of the world.) The complexity of flavor cannot be accounted for by a mere listing of ingredients: corned beef, sauerkraut, melted cheese, rye bread. Flattened and fanned out over most of a large platter and delicately crisp as the very best pizza, was there ever a Reuben like this at Reuben's? Let those who will try the Monte Carlo: corned beef and melted cheese dipped in egg before submitting to the buttered grill. With either, a good, zippy potato salad that tastes just made, and a bit of pickle. You won't miss a thing if you skip the homemade snapper soup; ditto the homemade pumpkin pie. Neither approaches the standard set by the masterbuilder's sandwich. As for the *arroz con pollo*, it's anybody's guess. The price of amateurism is unevenness, but better that than the homogenized blah's of more professional food mills.

The neo-Colonial décor doesn't measure up to the architecture, but on a cold day there are real enough fires in the large fieldstone fireplaces and a real enough flower or two at the table on all days. Look there. Also the murals over the mantel in the green dining room are by Karl Ritz of *Esquire* fame and they're charming. Look there.

> Ringoes Steak House, *Old Rte. 202 & Old Rte. 31, Ringoes, N.J. 08551. Located at edge of town, about 6 mi. from Flemington. Delores & Dick Yorke, Prop. L–12.30-2; D–5-9 Mon., Wed., Thurs., Fri.; till 10 Sat., 3-8 Sun. Closed Tues. BA, MC. Phone: 201-782-9018.*

Another out from Flemington: leave by Main Street (Route 523) and head for Stockton. (From Ringoes take the enchanting Ringoes-Sergeantsville Road.) Find yourself in rural America before the twentieth century. The capitol of this pocket country is SERGEANTSVILLE (pronounced Sir-gent as in detergent the townsfolk are swift to tell you, intolerant as any Parisian with the mangling of the language). Sergeantsville is unfake, unspoiled, if not altogether unselfconscious. And exactly at the "x" sits the very model of a tavern-by-the-side-of-the-road, the

---

SERGEANTSVILLE INN
Sergeantsville, New Jersey

LATE EIGHTEENTH CENTURY for the most part, it was excavated stone by stone from the years of neglect and the many misguided remodelings by the owners. They chipped and blasted away both inside and out, like dedicated archeologists. (This enormous labor is lovingly recorded in a scrapbook for your inspection.) The unclassy, unreconstructed knotty pine barroom where the local populace have been putting away quick ones for years gives way to the tiny, romantic stone-walled dining room and this to the even tinier Pandora's box. Forty is a full house here. The fireplace is not merely cosmetic as in

so many overheated dining rooms; winters, it works busily to cancel
the cellar coolness and trickles of arctic air that tunnel through the
chinks. To warm you further, there are the wines. The root cellar has
been surprisingly well-stocked, not of course with the turnip and the
potato but with the fruit of the grape. Resident wines date back to
the '60's and even the '50's. Here's an Haut Medoc and a Meursault-
Charmes—both '62's, a *very* good year. And the prices for such vanishing species are relatively light. To accompany these unusually
fine wines there is only peasant food dominated by Italian specialties.
However, the spaghetti sauce is made from scratch with fresh tomatoes, and "mom's" desserts are worth whatever they cost in calories,
since the "mom" they mean is the one responsible for the desserts
at New Hope's Tow Path in the Tow Path's golden years. Try her
pecan pie and you'll be in a forgiving mood.

If there's enough daylight left, proceed to Stockton on Route 32
using your horn as you go theough GREEN SERGEANTS, New Jersey's
last covered bridge, and keeping your eyes open for a look at ROSE-
MONT, another pure-hearted village.

> Sergeantsville Inn, *Rte. 523, Sergeantsville, N.J. 08557.
> Located 4 mi. from Stockton, 9 mi. from Flemington.
> Mabel & Michael Pittore, Prop. L—11-2 Wed.-Sat.; D—
> 5-9.30. Open Sun. 2-10 but subject to change—check first.
> BA. Phone: 609-397-3286.*

Restaurants are something like neighborhoods or rock bands.
They age poorly. According to one restaurant collector of note, the best

and the healthiest have fifteen good years. Then some essential ingredient seems to go out. An invaluable employee dies or hits the bottle or a chef leaves in a dudgeon over some corner-cutting in the kitchen. The owner sells out to a syndicate or stays too long at the track. Anyhow, Mother Colligan isn't around anymore to cook up marvelous dishes for the starry names that buzzed around

COLLIGAN'S STOCKTON INN

Stockton, New Jersey

YES, THIS IS the small hotel Rodgers and Hart had in mind when they wrote "There's a Small Hotel." The well is still here, banking money, and the waterfall and the charm and the crowds. Especially the crowds. They queue up in summer in order to eat out on the dappled terrace under the trees, and in winter in the older, choicer front rooms where walls still wear marvelous old amber-hued murals painted by some unheralded primitive and fires crackle and pop in the fireplace behind glass curtains so as not to cook the guests.

A staunch fan says she drives here frequently after church for Sunday dinner and—woman alone on this family day—feels warm and welcome and well-fed in about equal parts. Romantics love the romance—and the thick prime ribs—in that order. A mellow couple at the next table have been eating here happily twice a week for the past **forty years** hovered over by the same well-aged waiter, Carl, from the Golden Age of Bucks County. They, too, have been hitting the roast beef rather hard and feeding a lot, one suspects, on memories.

Only, maybe, the bees and the aphids give a damn that the flowers tumbling off balconies, tumbling out of hanging baskets under the trees or set piously in all the niches never need watering. Only small minds would quibble that neither the "famous" brace of quail nor the partridge listed on the menu in the menu's game preserve is available; one can, after all, make do with venison. *Tsk*—the turkey is dry, true, but whose isn't? No amount of slivered almonds would put snap back in those beans, but where can you get vegetables cooked to order these days? If the touted German chocolate cake with kirsh and whipped cream is once more unavailable, think of the calories you save! The brothers Colligan (minus Eddie who skipped out and opened Cuttalossa Inn across the river) have made several millions it is claimed. Not being greedy, they are content to rest on their laurels.*

There is a notable wine cellar on these premises, be advised. Atten-

---

*In late winter, 1974, the Stockton Inn was sold. The new owner's plan to restore the hotel part of the inn and, with luck, they may do as much for the cuisine.

tion must be paid to a restaurant with a treasury of '66 Burgundies . . . a restaurant with such charm the customers couldn't care less about the food. If you come, have beef 'n' burgundy, say a '66 *Nuits St. Georges.*

> Colligan's Stockton Inn, *Main St., Stockton, N.J. 08559. Located 5 mi. N of Lambertville on Rte. 29. Guy L. Gerhart and Mildred B. Fitzpatrick, Prop. Open daily in summer: L – noon-2; D – 5-9.30, till 10 Sat., 1-9.30 Sun. In winter D only. Closed Mon. Phone: 609-397-1250.*

You can't, it seems, have it all. If Colligan's and Sergeantsville Inn have the wines, there is a restaurant down by the railroad tracks in that same little village of Stockton with the food that deserves them, but no license. Small matter. Fetch something from the well-stocked WELSH'S LIQUOR STORE in Lambertville, long a resource for wines, and come straightwith to

---

MICHAEL SHORT'S RENAISSANCE

Stockton, New Jersey

SURELY THE ROOM is too unusual, too consciously "done"? From exposure one learns that the best food is often served in banal settings (though this hypothesis doesn't work the other way . . . banal décor is no guarantee of good food); it's as though one sense had been developed at the expense of another. Here, hanging plants dawdle in the windows and they are all *live*, a suspicious circumstance in itself! Hanging lamps – plain round globes covered with little dark red shawls – drip fringe and light on bare and glowing dark brown tables, rather *mysterious*-looking tables. These are set with branching candelabra and a small army of empty wineglasses and brilliantly flowered napkins like bouquets.

In the middle of the room, half-hidden by a wrap-around counter of black and white squares, is our host in his live-in kitchen. As he said later, he accommodates no more than forty at a sitting so he can handle the whole operation himself, "so I can control it." Menus are chalked up on a blackboard and hung on the rough plaster walls: scampi . . . beef *stroganoff* . . . roast duck *bigarade* . . . turkey *tettrazini*. There are four offerings nightly and except for the duck, a standard, they change from day to day. (If it's beef Wellington, it must be Thursday!)

For starters, *escargots provençale*, packed, stuffed, jammed to the rafters with a mash of garlic and shallots and herbs — not for tender-feet, not to be undertaken alone except by misanthropes, not to be missed. Onion soup is deep and brown, gratinéed under the broiler and brought to the table still bubbling. The salad, an arrangement of greens with long slivers of mushrooms and avocado, has the best oil-and-vinegar dressing in memory. Beef stroganoff struggles with an overdose of cream and needs salt — these things will happen on a Saturday night. But the scampi is grand, and the prune-stuffed duck sufficiently grizzled to be eaten skin and all. Broccoli in lemon-y butter is cooked *à point*, a miracle among others this night. His recipe: green stalks, parboiled, are popped under the broiler for a last-minute heating and buttering — as simple as that.

Sherry trifle is offered up in a large bowl, a fascinating complexity of flavors with a raspberry base. Unforgettable. There's also a raspberry meringue glacé, a chocolate mousse, and fresh strawberries-in-January with cream. The smashing espresso made two by two in one of those infernal old-world machines is the best this side of Italy.

By the end of the meal, it struck us as the most beautiful table we have ever spilled wine and crumbs on. Is it possible to buy one like it? It is indeed, our waitress assures us. Michael makes the tables, too. They can be ordered anytime if you have the ante, $1,200. Dinner is less: $11.00, including tip, and a bargain. Both are works of art.

Michael Short's Renaissance, Bridge St., Stockton, N.J. 08559. Located 5 mi. N of Lambertville off Rte. 29 near the bridge. Michael Short, Prop. D — 6.30-midnight Wed.-Sun. Closed Mon. & Tues. Phone: 609-397-9818.

Still another possibility: Point north up River Road (Route 27) from Stockton or take Route 12 west out of Flemington and, in the latter case, stop when you see directly in front of you a sign reading:

FRENCHTOWN NATIONAL HOTEL
Frenchtown, New Jersey

FRENCHTOWN IS WORTH poking about, the almost European triangle of shops in the heart of things, the Carpenter Gothic houses down the sleepy, shady streets. A proper river town. The National, just off the square, is the best hotel in town—*again*. The handsome three-story building was put up in the 1840's. In between is a tale of slip and slide and sloth . . . "lounge lizards" and pool sharks and rummies occupied the premises. Not a place you'd take the family for a Sunday dinner or put up a visiting relative. Probably the only thing that kept it from complete self-destruction are stone walls thick as a man's forearm: during remodeling it took one and a half days and three electric drills to make a hole in the wall. Though the place is cleaned up now, and painted, and prettied with motifs like cabbage roses, the pool table still sits in the barroom in a position of honor, and former habitués need not feel entirely dispossessed. But the dining rooms with their stained glass panels over the entrance (not put there by the hand of any *living* decorator) are almost genteel. The kitchen has been turned over to the preparation of no-nonsense steak and chicken and sea food and chops and Greek specialties, a rarity on the banks of the Delaware. The new owner and the chef both arrived here by way of the S.S. *Amerikanis* and the S.S. *Chandris* bringing with them *shish kebab* and rice *pilau, moussaka*, memorable hot stuffed mushrooms, Greek antipasto or Greek salad, hot shrimp with feta in a wine and tomato sauce. All very reasonable, too—take the kids.

Frenchtown National Hotel, *29-31 Race St., Frenchtown, N.J. 08825. Located 11 mi. W of Flemington via Rte. 12. John Tetteris, Prop. Open daily for L—11-3, D—5-10, from 7 Sat., from 12 Sun. Breakfast Mon.-Sat. AE. Phone: 201-996-4891.*

CLINTON

INNS AND OUTS

LISTEN TO THIS: at the point where the South Branch of the Raritan River and Spruce Run Creek meet there's a sheet of falling water nearly 200 feet wide from shore to shore, anchored at either end with an old mill. For a backdrop, whitish limestone cliffs, a willow tree that leans down and tests the water, a path that whisks around a bend and disappears. Scattered here, there over this watery landscape are Muscovy ducks, some swans, mallards, geese. They nest just offshore visible as decoys among the clumps of rushes, or swim off this way, that, inexplicably, or closing ranks and approaching on foot, demand handouts. Dear Reader, you are in CLINTON, New Jersey, and the time is now.

Closer inspection will not turn up a sweater barn or a canning factory or a mill-end shop. This gentle, pastoral scene that roots Clinton securely in its own past is a park. The old red mill with the water wheel is the CLINTON HISTORICAL MUSEUM with three floors of well-staged exhibits of Early Americana. Typewriters and telephones and bicycles and a commendable collection of lighting devices as well as the more often met with farm tools and spinning wheels, butter churns and china. Taking to the path you'll come upon a nineteenth-century blacksmithy and on Sundays, a twentieth-century blacksmith. A little farther on in another little outbuilding there's a convincing recreation of an old country store complete with post office and barbershop. A gift shop is tucked in here, too.

76

The mill across the water – a large, dignified stuccoed stone building with gambrel roof – was an active grist mill right up to the 1950's. These days, it's an active community center for arts and crafts, the HUNTERDON ART CENTER. When you get tired of feeding the water-fowl or paddleboating cross the bridge and look in. There are eight exhibitions a year of both professional and amateur work and the museum is especially hospitable to the crafts – the usual potting, weaving, jewelry-making as well as the not-so-usual glassblowing or a show of quilts. There may be a chamber music concert going on if you arrive on the right Sunday afternoon; at other times a lecture or movie or dance program on the little mill-race stage.

If you have a weakness for nineteenth-century architecture you've come to the right town. Walk up Leigh Street where a delightful procession of Greek Revival and Carpenter Gothic houses climb the hill on both sides uninterrupted by a single gas station or pizza parlor.

But this isn't getting you any closer to lunch. If you're hungry and don't want to leave the scene, retrace your steps, recrossing the iron bridge, and you're on the great-grandfatherly hitching-post porch of the

CLINTON HOUSE
Clinton, New Jersey

THIS IS AN EARLY stage coach stop and watering place of impeccable ancestry (c. 1743). The best view of the building is from the street where there's no sign of the heavy hand of the remodelers. Go straightwith to the taproom with its low wooden beams and a bar made of old beer kegs. The fireplace, predictably enough, doesn't work, and centuries of soil have been imprisoned under cheap varnish, but there's no office panelling or hotel lobby carpeting here, at least.

The waitress lobbied for the prime ribs, the indisputable favorite of waiters and waitresses wherever you happen to be. "But not like ours," she protested. They **do** get the very best raw materials at Clinton House, we have on good authority. If you don't mind paying for it, you can obtaine *terrine de fois gras à la Strasbourg* with truffles or Beluga Malassol caviar, a *Chateaubriand** or crown of lamb* or a *bouillabaisse.** It's just that all too frequently something happens to the food on the way to the table. But it is a good lunch or drink spot. This day, a prosaic cream of mushroom soup but a nicely upholstered turkey sandwich. Or potato pancakes (typically they could have been crisper) with applesauce and bacon. Desserts lean heavily on ice cream, a classic listing, plus two or three unavailable baked goods. The service is excellent.

> Clinton House, 2-4 W. Main St., Clinton, N.J. 08809. *Located between Somerville & Phillipsburg off I-78 (Clinton-Pittstown exit). Oscar Zierer, Prop. Open daily year-round. L—noon-2.30; D—5-10, till 11 Sat., 1-9 Sun. AE, DC. Phone: 201-735-5312.*

We all know how prophets go unhonored at home, but something like that seems to be the case with restaurants, too. When dining out, few people are content to stay in their own backyard, and except in the vaguest way, no one in Clinton had even heard of the best eating in the whole area or where to find the splendid

BRUNNER'S LANDMARK
Clinton, New Jersey

NOT THAT IT'S EASY. [Leaving Clinton, go north on Route 31 to the upper end of Spruce Run Reservoir—it's two miles from Route 78. When you reach the turn-off, Van Sickles Road, there'll be a light. Make a left and drive around the fingery fringes of the reservoir ¾ of a mile till you come to two stone gateposts.] The house waits at the top of the hill at the end of a tree-lined drive, a self-important white Victorian affair that looks like the kind of place where the underworld likes to gather and divide up the world. All mystery evaporates, however, upon entering this most bourgeois of homes: the Brunners are Swiss. There are tables and a fireplace in the sitting room and in the dining room, and more tables in the parlor and on the long porch where the view is served up at every window: the downsweeping lawn with its stands of weary old Norwegian pines and beyond, the blazing blue water of Spruce Run.

Close your eyes to the décor, the institutionalized bad taste of a generation past. When the food arrives, you forgive it all—sentimental prints, sickly-scenic plates, Roxy-like sconces. For the food is good. Very, very good. Onion soup, while not gratinéed, is a full-bodied, dark gold brew with a raft of toast on top, cheese on the side. The salad, passing fair, doesn't alert you for what's to come: probably as perfect a quiche as you'll meet in a lifetime. A large wedge of fluffy, cheese-y custard with nuggets of ham and bacon, a lunch-in-itself though you'll find it under "appetizer" on the menu. The crust is rich, flaky yet substantial. For dessert, there is the very Swiss emphasis on ice cream, homemade pies (judging by the quiche, these should be Something), cheese cake and a caramel custard topped with whipped cream, the winner and it is. Heavenly stuff.

The simplicities of lunch merely set you up for a dinner visit (though it would be a shame to miss the view . . . come early). Then the plot is more complicated. The menu is three pages with a special chapter on seafood. You can eat Swiss here (*rahm schnitzel* with noodles . . . minced calves' liver in a Madeira sauce . . . Swiss apple fritters) and you **should**, at least for the first visit. Be warned, however: the cheese fondue for two with a bottle of Neuchâtel and coffee at $15.00 is not priced for peasants. The quiche, at $1.75 is.

Don't come on Tuesday or Wednesday. Landmark is closed on those days so Anton Brunner, who apprenticed at the Restaurant Kronenhalle in Basel and isn't yet hooked on speed and efficiency, can make the homemade stock that goes into the sauces and the soups, and dozens of other preparations there isn't time for during the week.

Brunner's Landmark, *Van Syckel's Rd., Clinton, N.J. 08809. Located at top of Spruce Run Reservoir off Rte. 31. Tony & Trudy Brunner, Prop. L—noon-2; D—5-9, noon-8 Sun. Closed Tues. & Wed. AE. Phone: 201-638-6585.*

VII.

UP THE DELAWARE

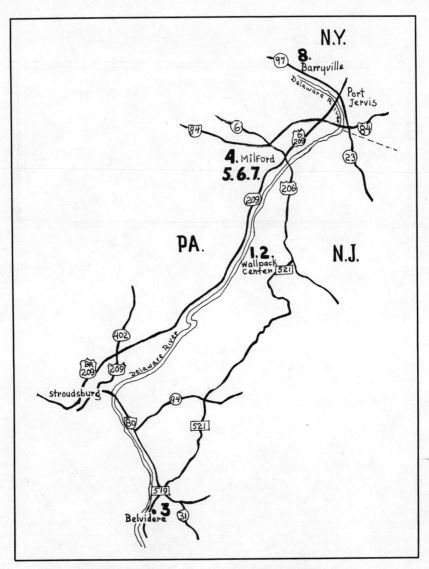

1. WALPACK INN
2. SLEEPY VALLEY FARM
3. LANARK INN
4. HOTEL FAUCHÈRE
5. CLIFF PARK INN
6. THE – – INN
7. PAUL'S BAKERY
8. REBER'S

Transit companies serving the area: Bus from N.Y.C. – Short Line (Milford, Penn.); Bus from N.Y.C. *or* Phila. – Pocono Mountain Trails (Milford, Penn.).

WEST JERSEY
ODYSSEYS

THERE'S A LOT of country left in the country, even so. Take West Jersey. It still consists of half rolling and even pitching farmland with the HUNTERDON HILLS to the south and in the north the KITTA- TINNYS, a part of the Appalachian chain, herded against the sky. Just as Monmouth has a concentration of race horses, Sussex has the show horses and come August they are paraded at the largest horse show in America. At GREAT GORGE there's more skiing than anywhere in the Poconos; it's not the Golden West nor yet Vermont but it has that love-able quality when you live in the mid-East of proximity.

There is a scholarly dispute over the origin of the name WALLPACK, the tiny hamlet on the edge of the floodplains just below STOKES STATE FOREST in northwestern Sussex County. One faction holds it comes from the Indian word for whirlpool, another from the Dutch "wal-peek" meaning deep water. Whirlpool or deep water, Wallpack is prophetically named. The mind-boggling and bitterly fought recrea-tional lake planned for this region in conjunction with Tocks Island dam will put much of the area under water. Water, deep water, will straighten Wallpack bend, a remarkable coil of river, as it covers the rich farmlands of the surrounding plains and sinks the hills to their knees. Water is the wave of the future for much of the OLD MINE ROAD, built by the Dutch in the seventeenth century to transfer copper from the Pahaquarry mines down around the Gap up to Esophus, New York. Water will bury an old Indian graveyard and rebury an Indian dig* where arrowheads that go back to 1400 have been un-

*Boehme Farm.

83

earthed. No one is exactly certain what is written in the water for Wallpack Center. A bridge, some headstones, a house or two, perhaps, and, of course, the valley. There'll be motor boats scudding over the misty, billowy green valley that comes to within yards of

WALPACK INN
Wallpack Center, New Jersey

... BUT NOT JUST YET. Come early.

West Jersey would not be losing an important *historical* landmark if the lake waters rose and claimed this place too, but it is expected to survive the floods and the present owners plan to lease it from the government. The origins of the inn are buried deeply under many renovations; all that's known is that the present owners, the Heisers, are in their second generation at this stand, pushing back walls, pitching in. A passion for collecting has paid off handsomely. Using tools and artifacts from the past, walls have been made into still-lifes ... old lanterns light windows curtained in recycled Agway feed bags ... waiting guests sit on pews. In one dark corner there's a Victorian pump organ.

Jimmy, Jr., commutes to Aspen where, according to Craig Claiborne, some of the best eating between New York and San Francisco is to be found, and he's taken careful notes. The salad bar, an institution which may very well have started in Aspen, is splendidly stocked without getting silly about it (no, no Bac-o bits) and the greens held forth in the great-grandfather of copper bowls sunk in ice. Stupendous rounds of a remarkable Scandinavian rye with a crust hard as a fist is baked on the spot every week, and served with big slabs of cool sweet butter. Dinner arrives: lamb shish kebab in an untimid baptism of wine and herbs, blistered a beautiful mahogany under the broiler. An outsize potato, perfectly baked, comes with it, but tonight carbohydrate counters will work on the bread or save themselves for dessert — or both. Dessert is *not* dismissable. Jimmy's mother is famous for her pies which she makes with fresh uncooked fruits like peaches or grapes or blueberries and covers with a delightful glaze.

There's a clambake tonight in the back yard. A real one with the classic fixings: lobsters and clams, seaweed, hot rocks and a tarpaulin to stretch over the pit. With it, charcoal-broiled chicken, corn in season, unlimited trips to the salad bar, sherbet and coffee for $8.95, complete, provided you've made a reservation in time. If you haven't, take comfort in surf and turf together or separately or teriyaki steak or various sea food and chicken dishes. Saturday, there's an enormous side of beef turning on an open spit. It **must** be good, for all the guests need come from miles and miles away. There's not too many hangers-around in this valley anymore.

Walpack Inn, Wallpack Center, N.J. 07881. Located near the southern tip of Stokes State Forest off Rte. 206. The Heiser family, Prop. Open in clement seasons for dinner only—5-9 Wed. & Thurs., till 10 Fri., till 11 Sat., 1-9 Sun. Closed Mon. & Tues. Rock Bake, Fri. 7-10 by reservation. Phone: 201-948-3890.

It looks more like Ireland than the United States, more like New England than New Jersey, Wallpack Valley. The greenness, the lushness, the all but tangible mists, the gentle rise and fall of the fields, the occasional outcroppings of rock. Then the lovely, lonely grey stone farmhouse at the bend of the road, at the End of the Dream—

SLEEPY VALLEY FARM
Wallpack Center, New Jersey

IT WILL NEVER HAPPEN, the del Russo's say, with finality, of the projected flooding of the valley. You hope they are right, if not for their sake then out of simple greed. The del Russo's serve dinner Saturday evenings only, only to the lucky few who have thought to book long in advance, and you are about to be turned away, empty-handed, empty-bellied. But look around, do. Cooking done with this much flair is, in part, a spectator sport anyhow.

So take your fill of the house with the beautiful bones, built originally in 1811 by an early Dutch settler, rescued and most respectfully restored by the owners. Antiques picked up on both sides of the Atlantic over the years have settled in, and guests, instant royalty, share the antique Spode, the old pewter plates, the English hallmark silver. There's a blaze in the hearth on all except the hottest summer nights.

For a preview of dinner wander through the garden-in-the-refrigerator. Each exquisitely slender green bean the exact length of the next, two and three-quarter inches, and of course taken from the garden out back. Backyard bib lettuce or maybe Belgian endive chilling together with glass salad plates. (The del Russo's not only make their own purist salad dressing, they make their own tarragon vinegar!) Cucumber soup and sorrel soup, cooked ahead, are "ripening" in the refrigerator. (In winter real Yankee bean or onion soup—they're ladled directly out of the crocks they're cooked in at the table.)

Only the best of the best is even tolerable on these premises. The main course is likely to be a roast shell of beef purchased directly from a New York wholesaler and "absolutely superb." The overriding importance of good raw materials is a religion. Anything Anne del Russo cooks is cooked with pure sweet butter and you feel the contempt she holds for anyone so benighted as to use anything less; in this kitchen cholesterol is a four-letter word. Freshness is a passion — fruits, vegetables, herbs (there's an herb garden in back); even the coffee beans are freshly roasted and ground.

A first course might be *jambon persillade en gelée* or roasted peppers with pine nuts, raisins and garlic, a cheese *soufflé* or a *shrimp quiche*. Cheese comes with the salad. Bread is homemade, served hot. For dessert strawberries or raspberries in season, steeped in liqueur, or maybe a *dolce Farinasi* (a ground almond and bittersweet chocolate loaf), a biscuit *tortoni* or a lemon chiffon pie. Then, always, espresso in sugar-edged crystal glasses.

When you come bring your own wine and aperitifs — your hosts will provide set-ups and ice — and plan to spend the whole evening as if you were going to someone's house. You **are** going to someone's house.

> Sleepy Valley Farm, *Wallpack Center, N.J. 07881. Located in deep country S of Stokes State Forest. Anne & Robert del Russo, hosts. Sat. evening dinner May-Nov. by advance reservation: 201-948-4883. BYOB.*

Next to the meeting house, the inn or tavern was the most important institution in the colonies and all highways started at a tavern or ended at one, a civilized custom. Think of it enviously as you penetrate ever deeper into the wilds of West Jersey getting hungrier and hungrier. There are few restaurants of *any* description in a wide swath of the map from Reigelsville on the Delaware north to the New York border until you come to a traditional inn with a tradition of good food, the

---

LANARK INN
Belvidere, New Jersey

OVER 200 YEARS AGO, looking a lot humbler and dustier than it does today, the Lanark was a stage stop between Newton and Easton. It isn't en route to anywhere much anymore. BELVIDERE, the Warren County seat, a sleeping beauty of a town that remains delightfully unimproved, is a bit farther north. Once a center of river trade when the Delaware River was U.S. 1, Belvidere's chief claim to fame these days is the old county courthouse on the village green and the canoe races each June starting at nearby Foul Rift. But don't wait for the races. Lanark customers come here from wherever they come expressly to eat. Follow their example. The food is exceptional, even if the décor is by Muzak, and the drinks have heft.

Soups are homemade so take the plunge—a fine nourishing bowl of vegetable soup, which despite its humbleness is one of the most difficult soups to bring off. On to Swedish meatballs, so light they fall apart when you even *point* a fork at them. There are lingonberries on the side for zing, and for substance, *spätzle*, the charming German dumplings not served often enough in this country. Cole slaw, one good clue to a restaurant's integrity and taste, is springy and creamy, not the usual drowned pulp.

Desserts baked on the premises are well worth regretting, but later, *later*: an excellent apple tart and a truly superior cheesecake on a cookie underpinning. Recipes are well-kept family secrets not even shared with *Gourmet* magazine who have nagged the Lutz's for their spinach recipe in the past. Mr. Lutz confesses the seafood is always fresh, admits they cure their own meats ("You have to.") and considers the prime ribs the best thing they do. To judge by this sampling, Mr. Lutz is *much* too modest. Roast beef is fine in its place but when the chef can cook like this, this is not the place.

> Lanark Inn, *Rte. 519, Belvidere, N.J. (mailing address: RD 2, Phillipsburg, N.J. 08865). Located 3 mi. S of Belvidere and 7 mi. N of Phillipsburg. Kurt & Rose Moses, Prop. L—11.30-2, D—5-9 weekdays, till 10 Sat. Closed Sun. & Christmas. AE, BA, MC. Phone: 201-475-2030.*

For those who enjoy the passing scene as well as good eating here are a collector's half-dozen favorite byways in Warren, Hunterdon and Sussex counties, some of the most beautiful pastoral passages anywhere in the East. There are others, untracked here, waiting to be discovered. If strung out in a straight line, they add up to over 120 miles of backroads still worth exploring.

- Route 519 from Belvidere to Newton (28 m.), passing through HOPE, the failed Moravian village, now declared a National Historical Site. Continue north and northwest on 519 ignoring Route 206 as long as you have the time and the gas to do so.
- The road along the Muscontetcong River from NEW HAMPTON south to BLOOMSBURY and FINESVILLE, old milling towns all, on down to RIEGELSVILLE on the Delaware (23 mi.).
- Route 517 from Hackettstown south to OLDWICK, passing through the once-fashionable, still-charming spa called SCHOOLEYS MOUNTAIN (about 13 mi.). Take side trips to CALIFON, to COKESBURY and MOUNTAINVILLE (10 to 15 miles).
- Zigzag between Clinton and Flemington, avoiding Route 31 except to cross it, and visit the villages of HAMDEN, STANTON STATION, STANTON, and THREE BRIDGES. If time permits go on

south to NESHANIC STATION and NESHANIC, crossing the SOUR-
LAND MOUNTAINS to ZION where Eugene O'Neill and George
Bellows once spent a summer, and finally HOPEWELL, a vintage
American town (about 30 miles).

• Retrace the OLD MINE ROAD*, the oldest highway in the East,
which goes by several names — Route 521, Old Delaware Road,
River Road among them. Branch off U. S. 206 at Montague and
take 521 South. Generally you want the west forks — toward the
river — except in Flatbrookville where you take the south fork
to Millbrook. The PAHAQUARRY COPPER HOLES are 8 miles north
of Delaware Water Gap. The trip, one way, is 33 miles.

HOME TO
MILFORD, PA.

Is PARIS BURNING? Is Venice sinking? Add to that list of the condemned the name of MILFORD, Pennsylvania, never to be the same once the man-made floods of Tocks Island dam are unleashed.

There's special poignancy to this river bluff town that overhangs the Delaware a hundred feet below. Dignified old trees arch over the streets, giving benediction. Dignified old white houses—some serving as library or veteran's headquarters—sit back on their green croquet lawns, reluctant to enter the twentieth century. Every hotel and boarding house has its hydrangea bush, its sweep of porch, its hanging baskets. A little stone house built back in the early 1800's out of local boulders and taxpayer's money is the jail; petunias are planted in window boxes below the bars and a weathered weathervane flies above the cupula. It's a pike—for Pike County, of course.

Milford was the playground of the rich and famous from New York and Philadelphia who came to take the cool, heady air and the waters, and to admire the romantic wildness of the surrounding countryside with its glens, glades, bosky dells and well-staged waterfalls, its trout-leaping streams and woods running with deer. Pre-World-War I Milford was even a movie colony; Mary Pickford, Francis X. Bushman, Lionel Barrymore all made movies here before the West won out.

The land hereabouts was wrested from the Indians in the notorious Walking Purchase;* maybe that is why Milford, a boom town in the early 1800's, has had such hard luck. It was passed over by the railroad interests, then by the canal builders. Now, ironically, it has been discovered by the truckers who savage the town while waiting for Rt. 84 to be completed, a matter of a year or two. Someday soon, Milford will resume its natural carpet-slipper pace and when you come to town there'll be plenty of parking space. But don't wait for the trucks to roll on or the water to close in before stopping off at the old, and very dear

---

HOTEL FAUCHÈRE
Milford, Pennsylvania

WHEN DELMONICO'S was Delmonico's, chef Louis Fauchère left, taking the recipe for Lobster Newberg with him. He opened up this hotel in 1852. Five generations later, the hotel is still under the dominion of the same family, from senior sister Marie, eighty-six, who never left, to Anne in her seventies, who came back, to nephew Louis Chol who made puff paste as a child under the tutelage of the old chef, Cesar, as another child might play with a pinch of mama's pie dough. Today elephant's ears and croissants are still being made right on the premises. So far, change, like the river, stays away from these doors.

Anyone feeling nostalgic for a time one never knew can come home

---

*A purchase of land equal to the distance that could be covered in a three-day's walk was (presumably) negotiated with the Delaware Indians by William Penn. Unfortunately, he postponed the completion of the treaty and did not live to carry out the terms. A stakeout was set for September 19, 1737. Under a son, Thomas Penn, the "Indian Walk" was turned into a run, a race, and one more rape of the Indian.

Picked for speed and endurance, the white team may or may not have had a rendezvous with some horses that just happened to be hidden at a point up ahead. What *is* known is they covered nearly 65 miles in the agreed upon day and a half, going in a northwesterly direction. To link up to the Delaware, they proceeded to draw a line running northeast to the river, taking in the Water Gap and Minisink land, twice as much territory as would have been the case had the line run to the Delaware by the shortest route, as the Indians had anticipated.

to Fauchère's. Meet the parlor—endearingly, shabbily Victorian. Stiff-backed sofas and chairs, peer-glass mirror, slipper seat, Oriental rug and a grand piano. Not a reconstruction or an embalmment. Everything grew on the spot. Upstairs the rooms are overwhelmingly Victorian: armoires, beds, dressers. The favored flowering wallpaper, used for years, now, alas, unobtainable, is by Lloyd's of London.

We eat on the porch, the "new" addition which already exudes the perfume of the past—no Muzak, no air conditioning, no haste. Dark, half-lowered blinds and a press of trees lend the room a cool green gloom. (An early and unnatural death to the baskets of plastic fruits and cornflowers.) There is but one waitress. Marie or Anne appear occasionally with a perfunctory bowl of relishes . . . or go to fetch drinks—from the pantry! Make it last. At Fauchère's waiting is elevated to a style.

Oddly enough, the French connection is plainer at noon, when Louis IV takes over, than at night under the *ancien régime*. Midday even the sandwiches are made of French bread, omelettes are featured, the plain but perfectly dressed greens known as salad Fauchère accompanies entrées such as a pâté of beef . . . zucchini stuffed with seafood *au gratin* . . . broiled filet of sole, Chablis . . . smoked beef tongue with *sauce Madere*. A *sabayon chantilly*, no less, concludes the soup-and-sandwich lunch! But it isn't till dark that the kitchen produces its pride and joy, the original Lobster Itself Newberg. Elegant eating. For anyone seeking something else there is an unambitious bill of fare with no surprises. An occasional abberration like cherry soup is dismal. There are only two desserts and both of them are ice cream. While you have meekly submitted to the sauce-free strawberry meringue glacé the waitress is tempting another diner at a table nearby with a fresh peach sundae (not on the menu). Apparently some things are negotiable.

There are too many discrepancies, true. An otherwise proper French omelette has tarried too long in the pan . . . is dry beyond redemption. A boiled potato has been permitted to get waterlogged. Ice-water sparkles in a pitcher at the breakfast table, but the waiting juice is room-warm. There is only orange marmalade to spread on the elegant croissants. All the *vins* are *ordinaire*.

But, yes, go. Eating at Fauchère's has always been more than a meal, for heaven's sake, and now we have the dauphin making certain desirable changes slowly, gently. Lunch, in particular, is quite reasonable. In summer, bring your bathing suit and take a swim at the local beach on the green, tree-fanned banks of the Delaware. While it's there.

> Fauchère's, *401 Broad St., Milford, Pa. 18337. Located within walking distance of center of town. The Fauchère family, Prop. L—noon-2, D—6-8 daily. Closed Jan.-Feb. 14. Phone: 717-296-9930.*

After winding uphill and uphill some more, then easing out through a long tunnel of trees, the scene before you looks something like Heaven Revealed even if you don't play golf. It's

---

CLIFF PARK INN
Milford, Pennsylvania

BLUE-MISTED GREENS roll off on all sides into the waiting woods. Somewhere in the middle, the ever-so-familiar white farmhouse with green shutters and green screen door . . . a sleepy-time rocking chair veranda.

In the beginning—this goes back about 150 years—there was a tannery here, followed by a logging operation for the Erie Railroad. This last cleared the way for the present preoccupation, golf. It would surprise no one to look out and see guests stalking off in cap and knickers and argyles, armed with mashies and niblicks. Pre-World-War I, this was a place where the game was played in a gentlemanly way . . . in one's own front yard . . . in one's own good time. And, it still is, though the original nine holes are now neatly fitted into the first five and four more holes have been added.

It took five generations of Buchanans to create Cliff Park. The family history can be read in snatches on the walls, a portrait here, a letter there, the Buchanan seal, an 1860's Bible on a stand, and bronze castings of one Buchanan or another as chevalier . . . as Indian scout, occupy the mantels over the fireplaces. To see them you must move around great barrier reefs of stiff-backed sofas, self-important chairs and rockers, carved tables, secretaries, around bookshelves that revolve on a stand, and crystal-dripping glass lamps—a concentration of Victorian pomp. The rugs underfoot are honorable old Orientals. It is not entirely an accident that you feel like a guest of the family. The Buchanans, who presently live in Virginia, return each summer with their six children and this or that cousin or niece: star boarders all. They are presently adding five holes to the course (one a water hole modeled on Pebble Beach in California) as much for their own private pleasure, one suspects, as for the guests. To preserve the original lines of the house, unattractive accretions are being removed one by one, and one by one the plain but comfortable guest rooms are being prettied up, Victorianized. The most deluxe room has its own adjoining wicker-filled sunroom in addition to a royal bedstead and marble dresser.

Food, let it be said, is not the main event here, though Saturday night buffets starring ham and roast beef are very popular, and few guests stir very far on Fridays when they always serve steak and lobster. But if you should decide to try elsewhere, the management indulgently makes allowances. Since the inn is not open year-round, the kitchen has been an uneven operation, but the new manager feels that he now has that problem, like his slice, licked.

Strangely enough there are cliffs at Cliff Park. Enter the woods and civilization speedily drops behind. Deer live here in late fall—you can see them feeding at the edge of the woods—and the quick red fox. Ascending first ridiculously by golf cart, then by foot when the going gets rough, you arrive in a very few moments at the edge of the world. There is a peculiar cry in the wind and a hawk swoops up from below somewhere and hangs kite-like in the sky; eagles used to live along this crest, too, though none has been sighted in the past three years. Look down if you dare into the valley said to be 900 feet below, the Minisink Flats—careful!—where the Delaware snakes through what will be lake bottom if the engineers of Tocks Dam have the last say.

> Cliff Park Inn, *Milford, Pa. 18337. 1½ mi. beyond town on State Rd. (look for signs). Harry W. Buchanan, Prop. L–12-3, D–6-9, all day Sat. & Sun. Open daily May 30–Nov. 15. Lodgings. AE. Phone: 717-296-6491.*

This Milford enclave is lucky in several ways. It has a frenziedly busy bakery, PAUL'S, where it's a pleasure just to come and sniff.

That exotic smell in the air is butter. Everything here is baked with it. The glossy Danish, beautifully browned, keeps floating up from the rear on trays and tastes like Danish, flaky not cake-y, melting. It makes breakfast, served at counter or table, worth getting up for. Before summer people leave, they pack the trunk high with Paul's bakery boxes to feed the freezer when they return home.

Milford is also favored with a great restaurant, ferociously ambitious and absolutely fearless, unafraid to tackle anything from *haute* to *bas*, including French soul food. The owners, man and wife, are virtuosi of the first rank. She prepares the desserts and bakes the bread, and at dinner hour mediates between dining room and kitchen. He does everything else.

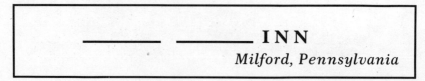

—————— —————— INN
Milford, Pennsylvania

NEVER HAVE WE EATEN ANYTHING remotely like the hot pig's knuckles *vinaigrette*, or as good. The shark's fin soup that follows is head-clearing . . . purifying with its intensity, as a good broth should be. Shrimp *aïoli* is shrimp revealed, not concealed, and will make you unhappy ever after the pallid and/or rubbery and/or iodine-flavored imitation. There are ten or twelve swoonable desserts including home-made chocolate triple *sec* ice cream, cherry *clafouti,* a chocolate torte with orange icing which is chocolate to the nth power. They could not improve on the fresh grapefruit sherbet sampled, made by hand with love . . . or could they? Anything is possible here. Even the bill which is under $10.

The next day you go back to the American Gothic farmhouse at the edge of the meadow. A painted cock on a pedestal at the foot of the steps unfreezes, jumps into a tangled web of flowers fighting it out in the way of French doorstep gardens. The proprietor is yanking a huge galvanized tub, the new lobster pond, into place. "It's not true," he says, at one point. "Not everybody can run a restaurant. You have to have a talent for it like anything else. Like music or pole-vaulting. A special talent, a special set of reflexes." You agree humbly. "I don't have a garden anymore. Too time-consuming. But in the spring we have a crop of morels under those elms. No. It would not be fair to our old customers if you wrote about us and we were to get deluged. All we want with this restaurant is our subsistence. That's about what it gives us—lets us live here."

There's no arguing with this mad, ungreedy Englishman or his beautiful, pale-haired Finnish wife who claims she cooks as she cooks because she is forever famished.

In the future they plan to be open only half of the summer. "The work! The work!" Honor compels this writer not to give name and address but from the clues provided a deserving reader will be able to dig up the address. Milford is a human-scaled town.

    _____ ____ Inn *(name withheld by request) is located in the country not far from Milford. Open all year for dinner only by reservation. Closed Mon. and (tentatively) July & Aug.*

WHITEWATER
AND SUDS

FOR MILES along the upper reaches of the Delaware River above Port Jervis there are more canoes to be seen than houses and the world, hushed by forests that come right down to the river's edge, looks new, gilded, just-created. In the East. In the United States. In the last quarter of the twentieth century. The river winds and unwinds, then dives between and around some hills, reappears minutes later, turns white as it squeezes through a narrow gorge, grows silky again. And so it goes for 75 miles. To make it interesting for the canoes, the water is strewn with riffles. In the spring, after the rains, its even *more* interesting. The banks grow distant, the river churns and turns brown and looks in a tremendous hurry. Every year a certain number of canoeists lives are exacted for the shuddering pleasure of taking on whitewater like SKINNER'S FALLS below Shohola.

Down around Trenton and below, this same Delaware River eats tippy canoes for breakfast due to the gunk from six of America's mightiest corporations. This far north it's still washed clean and the river's so shallow in places the temptation to wade across or walk on top from rock to rock is nearly irresistible. (*No dreaming, though, you in the canoe.*) There are also unexpected deeps, swimming holes and fishing holes that bass and walleye pike and sunfish and catfish call home, with one near Narrowsburg that descends 113 feet. Canoes can be rented ahead and delivered upriver to designated spots. The same company* will see that you have life vests and are reunited with your car.

*Bob Landers, Minisink, N.Y.: 914-956-8373, or Narrowsburg: 914-252-7101.

At Lackawaxen there's an old thrill for bridge collectors and/or canal buffs—what is probably the FIRST SUSPENSION BRIDGE in the whole world. It was built by John A. Roebling, who went on to produce the Brooklyn Bridge, and it supported an aqueduct carrying the Delaware canal across the Delaware River. This was in 1847. When the railroads came along, the aqueduct was removed, but the bridge remained, and it's been named a National Historic Landmark. Graceful as bird-in-flight it's not, but unforgettable in its stiff, clumsy way as the Pyramids. And still functioning.

Route 97 is not called HAWK'S NEST DRIVE without reason. It will take the average nervous driver a good half-hour to negotiate the eighteen glorious miles from Port Jervis to Bavaria-on-the-Delaware, or

REBER'S

Barryville, New York

THE LARGE CHALET by the side of the road is encrusted with traditional tiles. Steins in all sizes and shapes press up against the glass, with more inside. Reber's is a well-known, well-liked restaurant-and-hotel with an outcropping of small chalets nearby, the motel cluster.

The food is unfailingly professional (translate as never less than pretty good . . . rarely better than very good). *Sauerbraten . . . weiner schnitzel . . . knockwurst* and *bratwurst* . . . fresh pig's knuckle with sauerkraut . . . herring salad—the old-country favorites—are alive and well. So are restaurant clichés like surf and turf or the all-star prime ribs. The local hamburger is a tartare steak sandwich, and limburger and liederkranz are still allowed in the dining rooms.

The beer that can hold its own in such company is gushing forth in a non-stop flow at the bar. Löwenbräu, on tap, the gold and the amber. Not like dark beer? Find it—what? Oppressive! "A glass of dark Löwenbräu for the lady . . . on me." The bartender as it turns out knows something about beer. Pale is *interesting* but Löwenbräu dark is *beautiful*.

Cuckoo clocks and hunting trophies share wall space with the Reber's collection of paintings which they pride enough to light well. The largest and grandest is by Emmanuel Leutze, of Washington-Crossing-the-Delaware fame. At the entrance to the large dining room, desserts are displayed like works of art themselves, a bouquet of tortes, of *schlag*-wrapped cakes, powdered apple strudel, fruit *kuchen*. This is **good** peach *kuchen*, no if's, and's or but's, and getting harder to find than decent apple pie. The fruit's melted into the crunchy, crumbly cookie crust and faintly caramelized on top. Congratulations to Grandmama Reber who still produces this, as well as the strudel, in her kitchen.

The guest chalets are across the road on an eyrie and one or two offer spectacular views of the Delaware snaking back to Port Jervis. Each one is painted with a frolic-y mural and planted with flowers for *gemutlichkeit*. Inside, *gemutlichkeit* turns into something grander what with orange velvet chairs and creamy satin coverlets. One of the chalets, bigger than the rest, is a lounge where guests meet guests or meditate on the balcony or send the kids to play ping pong while they steal a nap. There's a pool too, to *prove* this is a proper motel, sitting coolly in the lush green grass just below the sky.

Reber's, Rte. 97, Barryville, N.Y. 12719. 18 mi. from Port Jervis on Rte. 97 N. Matilda Reber, Prop. Dining room open continuously 11-10, 11-11 Sat. Closed Tues. & Dec. 15-Feb. 1. Lodgings available. Phone: 914-956-6222.

VIII.

THE POCONOS —
UPS & DOWNS

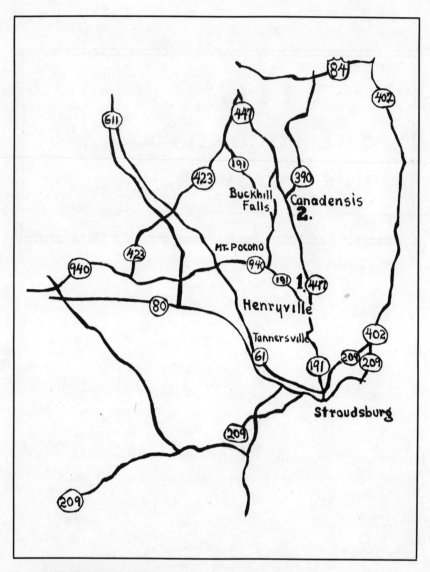

1. HENRYVILLE HOUSE
2. THE PUMP HOUSE

Transit companies serving the area: Bus from N.Y.C. *or* Phila. —
Pocono Mountain Trails (Henryville).

As mountains go the Poconos don't amount to much. 2,000 feet, maybe 2,200, down quite a way from their original 15,000 during the Devonian Age. Older than the Rockies, age has rounded them off, gentled them, greened them. They aren't the humbling sort with profiles that etch themselves in your marrow. Still, you sense you are up. The air, for one thing. Nights can be nippy even in July. If there isn't that much uphill, there is the downhill in winter in places like CAMEL-BACK and BIG BOULDER, more than enough to warm up on, snow conditions permitting.

Behind the billboards beckoning honeymooners hither with the latest motel status-symbol, heart-shaped bath tubs, there is another Poconos, most of it lying within hemlock-forested Pike County and it is very beautiful. Around BRUCE LAKE adjoining Promised Land and not accessible by car, there is virgin forest, hemlocks unmolested for three hundred years, bears hiding out in old rhododendron groves, and bears and other beasties rattling garbage cans at night. To keep things interesting, some rattlers too—it's best to wear boots. You'll need them anyhow if you hit the trail for any respectable distance as the stones can be brutal under sneakers.

For a sampling—something that can be done without benefit of backpack or any special expertise—try the APPALACHIAN TRAIL at the point where it crosses over from Jersey above Delaware Water Gap. If you neglected to bring lunch, have a whole wheat pizza on the back porch of OMEGA in the town of Delaware Water Gap. This is an old silver-shingled house turned health foods emporium located at the crossroads of this once-sought-out resort where you can taste the nostalgia. Where did the tall-hatted railroad magnets and the laughing opera stars, heads in clouds of chiffon, and the idle, no-good, beautiful-to-gaze-upon rich *go*? The Kittatinny Hotel overlooking the river burned to the ground, but other rich mausoleums remain, shells of themselves.

Sashaying around Stroudsburg with as much dispatch as is legal, trying not to hit the signs flagging you on all sides, pick up Route 191 which parallels what is said to be the best natural-spawning trout stream in the East, BRODHEAD CREEK. Ask Teddy Roosevelt. Or Calvin Coolidge or Grover Cleveland or Benjamin Harrison. Ask Annie Oakley and Buffalo Bill. They all cast here at one time or another, arriving by the Erie-Lackawanna Railroad and crossing over a hanging bridge on foot. When they did they stayed at

101

HENRYVILLE HOUSE
Henryville, Pennsylvania

SINCE THOSE DAYS, Henryville House has undoubtedly suffered a great fall, but it's coming back — well, *partway* back. Built in 1847 on the edge of a woods a few fly casts from the creek, it's perfectly suited to the role of hosting the fishermen who come *in schools* in the spring and now skiers in winter. With luck, one may snag the Presidential suite with its Victorian dresser and bed and needlepoint rug — the closest you can get to old Henryville style. Downstairs, the new owners are revamping the barnlike spaces into warm, welcoming rooms . . . . . . with a feeling for flowers. The wicker, revived with black paint and flowered cushions, is planted on the easy-going front porch along with hanging baskets of petunias. Flowers follow walks outside and wildflower-and-weed bouquets are invited indoors to charm the guests.

The summer dining room with a ribbon of skylight above is shaped like a pavilion and covered in a pavilion stripe. The food, however, is admittedly limited. In summer there is no attempt to do more than feed a lot of people with minimum staffing. The chef, almost unsupported, still manages great baking feats: delicious homemade doughnuts for breakfast . . . an acclaimed dinner bread . . . for dessert, open-faced sourcream apple pie as good as they come. The soup sampled, cream of chicken, has good, rich flavor. For a little extra he'll cook up your morning catch for dinner.

In summer this is a camp for families with children, teenage on down, and a kind of sub-camp for the undergraduates who work here dressed (or disguised) as waiters, desk clerks, chambermaids. Unless traveling en famille, come before mid-June or after Labor Day. Henryville's an inn for three seasons.

> Henryville House, *Rte. 191, Henryville, Pa. 18332. Located 9 mi. N of Stroudsburg, Pa. Bill Westover, Prop. Open Apr. 15-Oct. 30 by the week (mod. Am. plan), Christmas till Mar. 15 weekends only. Lodgings. BA. Reservations: 717-629-1688 or 800-221-9580.*

The official scenic route north from Stroudsburg is Route 446, but when the laurel is erupting in late spring *all* the roads are scenic. It really doesn't matter which way you go then as long as the road leads to

THE PUMP HOUSE
Canadensis, Pennsylvania

THE HOUSE is on a high ridge of the Poconos beyond the town. It has a pump, too, at the side of the porch, long since detached, but it keeps the name honest. There is a spill of people on the patio, more inside at the bar. The owner, pointing to a slate above the door where selections are listed, takes dinner orders and turns them over to the waitress in the wings; one of the nice customs in this part of the world is this civilized dawdling at the bar up to the last possible moment.

The Pump House, built in 1842, is a country inn with seven acres and a view as wide as the valley and high as the sky. There's a mellowness about it, a feeling for antiques and books and paintings and people, that you don't come upon very often. But the heart of this house is the kitchen from which only good things flow. The chef, Bill Caldwell, a graduate of the Culinary Institute in Hyde Park and of Stonehenge in Connecticut, once a holy place for gastronomes, is only 23-years-old. Even so, a driven man – *sérieux* as Drucquer *mère* says. (*Sérieux* is defined by food critic Raymond Socolow as the impelling need to do a thing "as if God were watching.") *Sérieux*, then, but also, *mon Dieu*, a man for us to watch, for he has the gift. The Drucquer family, the owners, are of French descent. Eating well is not something you save for special occasions; it's an ongoing, seven-days-a-week celebration of life itself as it is for great-grandfather's countrymen.

The summons comes and you are escorted through the parlor with its freshet of flowers in the silver champagne bucket, through the old dining room into the new. A wall of water at the far end streams over the "found" 40-ton boulder.

Forthwith, shrimps in beer batter, four monsters big as lobster claws, beautifully executed, served with a pungent fruit sauce undoubtedly of Chinese ancestry, and you're off. Spinach salad is bound up in a blue cheese dressing, strewn with raw mushrooms for a different kind of crunch. The rack of lamb *persillé* arrives, seven pink perfect chops seven, pinwheeled about a broiled tomato, gorgeously seasoned with crumbs. To support what needs no support, pan-roasted potatoes and fresh asparagus lapped in *hollandaise* – just two but each the astonishing thickness of a child's wrist and luscious end to end. The waitress comes forward with the inn's own mysterious and marvelous hot compôte, a mélange of fruits simmered in spiced wine. No element is neglected, not even the bread, the chef's handi-work, or the fresh, sweet crocked butter. It's "yes" to dessert, too. Not the sensible and appropriate pineapple steeped in kirsch, nor even the rich but refreshing strawberries Romanoff. No, a balloon of chocolate mousse! Or tonight's Black Forest cake swamped under whipped cream! Nothing exceeds like excess.

The rooms upstairs are little more than retiring rooms with private tiled baths or showers. If you stay up past eleven the bartender departs but he is too tender-hearted to lock up. Help yourself, and leave a con-tribution on the plate.

> The Pump House, *Skytop Rd. (Rte. 390), Canadensis, Pa. 18325. Located 15 mi. N of Stroudsburg, Pa. The Drucquer family, Prop. In season (June till early Oct.): D–5-9 Tues.-Sun. and Sun. brunch 12-2. Closed Mon. The rest of year D only Wed.-Sun. Closed Mon. & Tues. Lodgings. AE. Reservations highly desirable. Phone: 717-595-7501.*

IX.

A BUCKS COUNTY SAMPLER

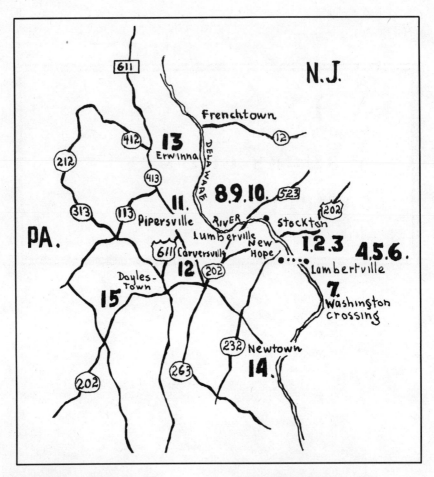

1. LOGAN INN
2. CHEZ ODETTE
3. RIVER'S EDGE
4. LAMBERTVILLE HOUSE
5. LA BONNE AUBERGE
6. GRACE'S MANSION
7. WASHINGTON CROSSING
   INN
8. BLACK BASS HOTEL
9. 1740 HOUSE
10. CUTTALOSSA INN
11. PIPERSVILLE INN
12. CARVERSVILLE INN
13. THE GOLDEN PHEASANT
14. TEMPERANCE HOUSE
15. CONTI'S CROSS KEYS
    INN

Transit companies serving the area: Bus from N.Y.C. – West Hunterdon Transit (New Hope, Lambertville, Erwinna/Upper Black Eddy) Bus from Phila. – Greyhound (Pipersville, Doylestown), Continental Trailways (Doylestown); Train from Phila. – Reading Railroad (Newtown, Doylestown).

NEW HOPE AND
THE NEIGHBORHOOD

LAMBERTVILLE* is a rinky dink river town, gutted in the middle by gasoline stations and dominated by a bridge crossing the Delaware into New Hope, carrying the tides of traffic and the tourists with it.

In Washington's time, Lambertville and New Hope were both referred to as Coryell's Ferry and, mill towns both, they shared the same history. But rivers, like railroad tracks, have a way of winnowing out the sinners and the poor from the more lofty and prosperous citizenry. In the Twenties, New Hope was colonized by artists and writers and theater people enchanted by the uphill and down dale countryside, by the indigenous stone houses, by the funny little town itself threaded by a canal and a railroad track and crisscrossed by bridges—a toy village.

New Hope may have been too successful. Visit it at your peril in the summertime. It's hot and it's crowded. There are too many scented candle shops, too much décor, and too few lavatories. But in the spring and in the fall and in the absolution of winter, the climate changes — it's not only cooler, it feels *real*. Natives stop snapping at the visitors and their no-necked children, and it's possible to sit down in a restaurant without queuing up first. The big annual art show at PHILLIP'S MILL is in October. The BUCKS COUNTY PLAYHOUSE** in the old Parry

---

*Located on the edge of Bucks County, in New Jersey's Hunterdon County.
**Between companies at time of writing, but expected to resume operations by Spring, 1974.

grist mill is likely to tackle more venturesome offerings in the off-
season than you'll find in the straw-hat season when it's always "Spring-
time for Henry." Now, while the village has shrunk back to normal
size and the local citizenry feel free to come out from behind their
houses and exercise their territorial prerogative, is the time to go.

The walking is plain wonderful. The walk of walks starts at Bristol
in Lower Bucks County and shuffles along the romantic TOWPATH
that stretches between river and canal till reaching Easton, fifty
miles later.* Lesser mortals can link up with the towpath at any point
that's convenient. Cyclists scoot along here too, unmenaced, as well
as poets, and in certain sections, horse and rider.** The canal itself is
hospitable to CANOEING, though you will have to negotiate the locks
on foot. If it all sounds like too much work, settle for a ride in a MULE-
DRAWN BARGE headquartered behind Logan Inn.

Shopping is the sport of sports here. This whole area, haunted by
history, is full of the detritus of the past: antiques. New Hope and
points south on Route 202 is lined with antique shops, a kind of
Third Avenue South, and the village of Lahaska is one big warehouse.
Acres of flea markets spring up weekends on River Road south of
Lambertville and on Tuesday mornings, there's Rice's Auction just
outside New Hope.

Smack in the middle of town, sitting back a bit from the street on
a stretch of lawn is an inn where Washington is known to have visited
and which it now appears may even have served as the General's
headquarters just before the crossing. In more recent history, it
served as headquarters for the Algonquin crowd. To sleep where
George Washington—or even a George Jean Nathan—slept isn't an
opportunity that presents itself every day in the week. It's the

---

LOGAN INN
New Hope, Pennsylvania

BLACK LEATHER CHAIRS are drawn up to the chirrupy fire in the wainscoted taproom, a study in browns, and everywhere you look—on the
walls, in the window reveals, on shelves, on the mantel—there are
collections: clocks, tankards, candelabra, antlers, pewter, bottles.
Behind the bar Arthur Sanders puts forth hefty drinks and sym-
pathy. He and his partner have taken over this place, which was little more than a barn when they moved in, where you had a quick one

*The canal is part of the Bucks County parks system. See the booklet available locally,
A Wayfarer's Guide to the Delaware Canal by Willis M. Rivinus.
**There's a 40-mile bicycle path linking nine state and county parks planned for Bucks
County and being opened up in sections at the present time.

(a very quick one) before the first curtain at the nearby Playhouse. You may eat here or in the crimson-flocked Victorian room where there is an unusually distinguished company of ancestors, real and borrowed, on the walls and a fine primitive. Or *sous cloche* in the courtyard, in the new stained glass greenhouse where it's always the middle of June.

Upstairs, great gorgeous carved Victorian beds sprawl across large, high-ceilinged rooms with marble-topped dressers and towering armoires. Every room has its own stamp and would make a splendid stage set: this is about as far as you can get from the nearest Holiday Inn. No phones. No television. The only nod to progress are private, tiled baths.

The chef who worked for years at 17 Barrow Street in New York, where all good Villagers went in the good old days, will only consent to cook "as he feels it." Vibration cooking, continental style. Back-stopping him is another accomplished performer in the kitchen, part-ner Carl Lutz, a kind of insurance that the guest gets what he or she came for.

Don't come here for dinner if all you had in mind was roast beef and baked potato. It would be a terrible waste where you find such special-ties as roast leg of veal *gourmand* (stuffed with pâté), or a *moussaka à la Turque* (beef-stuffed eggplant in a tomato and béchamel sauce), or a *cassoulet Toulousaine* (the classic version made with goose) or roast guinea hen *bonne femme*, a fine neglected game bird, simply cooked, stuffed with liver and caraway, and very tasty. The cook coasts through the rest of the dinner on his laurels. The modest prix-fixe desserts (tapioca pudding, pound cake, ice cream) give no hint of the extraordinary productions available à la carte. Like chocolate rum pie: very chocolate-y, very rummy, very very good, and weighed down with thick whipped cream. It would be hard to imagine a better way to let go unless it would be Logan's extraordinary buttercrunch chocolate cake, the layers bound by a luscious custard and the top crusted with a nut brittle. Or the grasshopper pie. All are baked on the premises—by the waitresses! All are best-savored by themselves in the late afternoon or after the theater. Weeknights there are five or six choices on a prix fixe dinner: Saturday the number of choices and the prices go up; appetizer and dessert are à la carte. Lunch is the usual.

> Logan Inn, *Ferry St., New Hope, Pa. 18938. Carl Lutz & Arthur Sanders, Prop. Closed Thanksgiving, Christmas, & New Year's Day.* Lodgings. *Phone: 215-862-5134.*

Downriver a short hop from New Hope is a French auberge lodged in a former barge stop of typical Bucks County stonework, very handsome . . . a local institution known as:

CHEZ ODETTE
New Hope, Pennsylvania

HAVE YOU ALWAYS secretly wanted to make a whole meal out of the marvelous morsels whisked about on appetizer carts and the devil take the rest of the meal? You can, you can. Have Odette's famous buffet lunch: a long table lavished with the classic repertory of cold meats, marinated cucumbers, French potato salad, ratatouille, onions *Niçoise*, vegetables *à la Grecque*—and some surprises like a whole cauliflower, marinated, a blush-green bouquet, or a spinach salad with a crumbly bacon dressing. In addition there are two main choices that change from day to day. It could be a hot beef salad (really a stew) or ham mousse with horseradish sauce or eggs in cream sauce. This day, lentils *Provençale* with blistery sausages and chicken *à la reine.* "Have both, you should have both. They're very good. The chicken is the same filling that goes into our *crêpes à la reine,*" urged the hostess in her Martinique accent, moving like a dancer as the spoons fly. It *is* delicious, this dish known as chicken à la king on the American mainland, and so are the lentils. No need to make painful decisions, unless you insist on ordering lunch from the menu: eggs Benedict,

Odette's *Salade Niçoise* (with shrimp), crêpe this and that. At dinner-time, in addition to the staples like *moules Odette* (mussels in curried mayonnaise), artichoke *vinaigrette*, king crab *à l'Américaine*, chicken *Kiev*, steaks, there are interesting specials that change nightly and are chalked up on a blackboard the waiter brings around. Lunch or dinner, don't skip the chocolate mousse which is moussier than most and almost enough for two.

The splendid buffet is within striking distance of the bar where the twilight is illuminated by a fire, wintry days, and Odette Myrtil can always be found after one o'clock. To her, this restaurant on the Delaware is not merely a livelihood, it's life itself. The toast of New Hope, she takes up her station by the bar with a friend at one elbow, a cane at the other, and a drink in hand, her poodles, two rugs at her feet. According to her friend the pianist, Stewart Ross, out of her musical comedy past, "We are in our comfortable seventies . . . and it works. This [New Hope] is her 'spiritual home.'" At night, he plays, she sings.

"Call me Odette," she says, taking a drink. "Everybody calls me Odette. Just don't call me 'Chez'! Imagine! They come up to me and call me 'At'," she adds gutterally, contemptuously, then guffaws in a split-second change of mood. This former discovery of Flo Ziegfield, the Bloody Mary of South Pacific, is Marlene Dietrich's rival behind the range. Three times a year she throws parties right on the premises, two open to the public. On July 14, Bastille Day, they fire away over the canal, and on Halloween there's a Beaux Arts ball, each year on a different theme and costumes are *de rigueur*.

This day sunlight beckons and if you're early enough you may find an empty table right by the water where the waterfowl put on a show that rivals Odette's. In passing, smile indulgently at the "Renoir" mural sweet as a Mont Blanc and at the general look of benign neglect. Keep your eye on the seagull—yes, a seagull!—lunching on the Delaware.

If you are rash enough to come here on a buzzing summer's night, bring patience and fortitude and snacks . . . you may not eat till the following noon. As it turns out, this is not the worst thing that could happen.

> Chez Odette, *S. River Rd., New Hope, Pa. 18938. Located at edge of town between river and canal. Odette Myrtil, Prop. L—12-3; D—6-10, till 11 Sat. Closed Sun., Thanksgiving, Christmas & New Year's Day. AE, MC, CB. Reservations essential Sat. night: 215-862-2773 or 2432.*

Two of New Hope's most famous restaurants are in Lambertville! Cross the bridge and turn left to go to

RIVER'S EDGE

Lambertville, New Jersey

A NIGHTTIME VISIT doesn't quite prepare you for the onslaught of this place, the charm. At night, the river is a river of darkness despite all the guttering candles. But a gilded day in late fall, it's a rush of blue water so close it seems to flow through the building, threading its way in and out of French windows opened wide on the world. An old grist mill (1835), it was rebuilt some years ago around a patio where flowers bloom non-stop. A golden pheasant steps around the chrysanthemums and a chukka partridge comes and goes while birds brilliant as butterflies splash around the aviary. A garden of delights.

The woman responsible for launching the original River's Edge, radio's "Stella Dallas," has now retired. A new team of chefs has arrived under the direction of John Walsh. The menu has changed, many say for the better, although the restaurant was *good* in the good old days. Superior things were *and* are done with sweetbreads here, or with crab. Soft-shelled crabs are sautéed respectfully and there are two or three of them, depending on the size. Also recommended is the inch-high slab of rare prime rib and the baked ham with champagne sauce. For dessert (mid-week), if you have the time and money, try the souffle *au grand marnier*. This specialty may disappear on the attenuated weekend menu. The coffee is elegant.

For a view of your own, make your reservation, as they say, early at river's edge or beside the fascinating comings and goings of the wild life in the outdoor aviary. And, if the mood strikes you right on a weekend evening, explore "The Club." This innovation of the new management is open until the early hours for drinks and dancing.

> River's Edge *on the Delaware, Lambert Lane, Lambert-*
> *ville, N.J. 08530. Just off Rte. 202 across the river from*
> *New Hope. John Walsh, Dir. Open year-round. L – 12-3;*
> *D – 6-11 Tues.-Sat.; 1-10 Sun. and on-into-the-night week-*
> *ends for dancing. Closed Mon. Phone: 609-397-0897.*

If Washington slept at the Logan Inn, as has been inferred, less than a century later Gen. Ulysses S. Grant and President Andrew Johnson rested and took refreshment at

---

LAMBERTVILLE HOUSE
Lambertville, New Jersey

ESTABLISHED IN 1812, and in operation ever since, bustling Lambertville House with its flowering balconies and iron balustrades has its partisans, like Colligan's down the road. The food is familiar. "Plain cooking" it's called, and some of it is not only plain but good; there *is* a difference. The management has hired a cast of local women to replace that tyrant in the kitchen, the professional chef, with varying results.

Dinner comes with portions that look swollen on lunch-sized plates, but the food is surprisingly tasty. Moist turkey with a modest but good stuffing of bread, celery and onions. Mashed potatoes with a reassuring lump in it to tell you these were not made from a box. Buttery lima beans. Someone in the kitchen loves oysters and treats them kindly with a thin skin of a crust and a hot, hot fry. There are only four but they are perfect. The same can not be said for the rather thin onion soup, the burnt-bottom loaf of hot bread, the oversalted salad or the fast-frozen parfait that won the contest with the spoon.

But the Lambertville House doesn't live by food alone. There is a bar of English descent that dispenses atmosphere along with alcohol and it's very popular. Upstairs, there are thirty-one rooms, three of which are truly sumptuous with kingsize beds and private baths and wall-to-wall carpeting, not to mention air conditioning and television. Down the hall is a little guest parlor furnished with antiques. The remaining twenty-eight rooms on the next two floors with their re-

versible fans in the windows and hot and cold running water and
communal bathroom should be saved for emergencies.

New Hope is just a bridge away but you may decide to stay with
Lambertville where the antique shops and the flea markets are a
shade less tourist-trappy than New Hope which was fine-tooth-
combed before you knew a hutch table from a table d'hote. Lambertville is a town ripe for discovery, and there are signs on some of the
back streets and up on the hills people are doing just that.

> Lambertville House, 32-34 *Bridge St., Lambertville, N.J.*
> *08530. John C. Allen, Prop. Open daily from 11.30-1 in*
> *the morning. L — till 3, D — till 10 (9.30 Sun.), late supper*
> 10-1 Mon.-Fri. Closed Christmas. Lodgings. AE, BA, MC.
> *Phone: 609-397-0202.*

High on a hill above New Hope there is a series of stylish condo-
miniums, tier upon tier, then another, then another, called Village
2. When you can go no higher you will have arrived at a charming
anachronism, a two-hundred-year-old fieldstone farmhouse. Inside,
there is another charming anachronism, the tradition of serving fine
food made exactingly to order by people who spare no labor or expense
to bring you the best. *Bien sûr*, you are at

LA BONNE AUBERGE
New Hope, Pennsylvania

UPON OPENING THE DOOR you are greeted by the just-released scent
of melting butter and a gust of voices and low laughter. Tables are
set up as if for a party in a private home: napkins tightly furled and
sticking straight up out of goblets like so many rabbits' ears, little
clutches of dried flowers stuck in small, sweet ironstone pitchers.

No one is here?

The room looks out on a glassed-in terrace and beyond that the
view you have just put behind you, the pretty winter-nude country of
Bucks County spread out obediently on all sides. Then the hostess
appears — from the waist up — at the top of the cellar stairs and, beckoning, winds tortuously down steps meant for the ridiculous feet of
Colonial sires and dames. We are in the root cellar, a small well-lit
cave of crumbly fieldstone shored up by a curious stone arch. A man
at the bar rears back to read the papers at arm's width, fearlessly, as
if he were at his own breakfast table. There is no hurry here . . . we
are in France, *n'est-ce pas*?

To read the lunch menu with its tuna salad, its Reuben sandwich, its grilled hot dog with bacon, you might wonder. Never at noon the rack of lamb *Arlésienne*, the chicken *grand-mere*, the veal *piccata*, and you must come back for dinner if you are to solve the stuffed shrimp *tartare*. (Answer: shrimp packed with crabmeat and herbs, then deep-fried.) *Potage cressonière* is the soup *de jour*, a real soup *de jour* since it's made afresh each day like it says, but **after** lunch.

And so the antipasto, which can mean anything from a wriggle of anchovy to a meal on wheels. At La Bonne Auberge, it's a *pique-nique* for a hearty eater or two lighter-weight ones—a prodigal platter of meats. There's pepper-pocked Genoa salami . . . many pink shavings of prosciutto . . . a whole slab of the delicious duck *pâté*. This is served with an icy cornichon, mustard and a nest of hot scatter-crumb rolls. It is difficult to hold back for the cheese omelette ordered earlier in a rash moment.

The omelette, however, is worth any sacrifice. It arrives sealed up in itself as it should be, all ooze inside as it should be, a perfect thing. Alongside, a pile of French fries, slender and crisp as swizzle sticks.

For dessert you pass over fresh cream cheese cake, a truly superb one it is rumored, light and fine and lemon-y, crisped with a delicate crust and shavings of almonds—a Coronello specialty. Save it for another trip, you tell the waiter who speaks no English yet. He nods. Linger at the home-made 151-proof rum *baba* before weakly ordering *crème caramel*. But this is no ordinary *crème caramel*. It is Mellow Yellow itself and lifts this dessert way out of the cliché class.

The owner-chef is too young and too handsome ever to look convincing to a casting director, but he has been training for this role since the age of sixteen, mostly in France, for he's half French. He has no use for the prepared foods that are the staff of life of most restaurants where even raw steaks are attractively branded with sear marks back at the meat plant so they'll look like a picture in the magazine when they're cooked and served. Tuesday, his day off, is the busiest day of the week, the day sauces and other lengthy cooking preparations take place.

"For what you **get**," his wife claims defensively, "our prices aren't that high. We buy **only** the best. This place only seats fifty people but the table you get is yours for as long as you care to stay." Not that high by New York standards, certainly. But not that cheap either. However if you find the lobster *à l'Américaine* on the menu it's worth whatever the cost, according to a famed cook.

The new owners have chalked up more than a year now in this spot, a long reign by local New Hope in-and-out standards. They've survived the Saturday night when the dishwasher disappeared and the bartender was besotted, and the hungry were fed mostly the tunes of the 'Thirties by the weekend piano-player. They just may decide to stay and tear up their return ticket to France. Serious eaters will want to investigate.

La Bonne Auberge, *Village 2, New Hope, Pa. 18938. Located off Mechanic St. in New Hope. Gerard & Rosanne Caronello, Prop. L — 12-2.30, till 2 Sat.; D — 7-10, 6-9 Sun. Closed Tues. & vacation (Sept. or Oct.) BA. Phone: 215-862-2462.*

About a block past the New Hope High School at the top of the hill, site of the former Toad Hall restaurant, there's a restaurant where ambiance is a dirty word and it's called

GRACE'S MANSION
New Hope, Pennsylvania

THE MANSION could have been a roadside hamburger stand before the hamburger moved up to classier digs. Or maybe an early (c. 1938) version of a diner. If it weren't for the straggle of colored lights and a wall of foreign cars including two Jaguars, two Mercedes, and one Rolls Royce convertible in front, it might appear abandoned.

Inside the décor is up to the standard set by the architecture. A counter. Some tables and chairs. Some posters left over from previous occupancies. And — unexpected note — a palomino-colored mastiff like a giant felled log across the floor. The Kresge milk glass vase with its one red rose and the clumsy cut-glass goblets set about on a white plastic "lace" cloth, the ordinary drug store tumblers provided for the elegant wine you dragged up from your cellar — all seems part of a plot, the final snub to the New Hope decorating establishment. But the food — **the food is beautiful**.

To begin, a buttery country *pâté* served with thin toast slices or fried mushrooms or oysters Rockafella. Then an onion soup of great substance, densely dusted with cheese and finished off in the oven. Fragrant, nut-sweet *veal scallopini* that succumbs to the fork. Or rich, luscious lobster crepes. Or prime ribs *mousseline* (painted with a zippy sauce and bubbled under the broiler). Broccoli *hollandaise* is cooked with respect, to order, and served with respect, separately. Overcome, no one notices that Grace who is blonde and attractive and abstracted behind her windowpane frames has forgotten to deliver the salad for which there is now no room.

Still you rally and order dessert. Can this act with its Vandermint mousse, its Black Forest torte, its strawberry cake-fall, its baked stuffed apple touch the same heights? It can. It does. The mousse lives in loving memory. The torte is overkill but a lovely way to go.

By contrast—and only by contrast—the strawberry cakefall (a cake roll with whipped cream and fresh strawberries) seems almost ascetic.

All entrées except the orange duck change from night to night, but with a track record like this just close your eyes and point. What you save in bar bill and décor and advertising makes dinner of this caliber sweetly reasonable (about $10 with tip). If the children are with you let 'em eat hamburgers at the counter; they'll be happier and you'll save even more.

> Grace's Mansion, 243 W. Bridge St., New Hope, Pa. 18931. Located in town next to high school on Rte. 202. Grace Wehmeyer, Prop. D only—5-9. Closed Wed. Phone: 212-862-2785.

Downstream six or seven miles from New Hope is another sort of village, one with a New England flavor, the place where Washington staged his most famous guerilla action against the enemy. Were this raggedy band to return they would have no problem retracing their steps, the old Ferry Inn where plots were laid, the embarkation point, the lookout hill (now marked by a tower), the mill that ground the grain for the troops and the miller's house. There they are still in Washington Crossing Park that runs along both sides of the river and preserves the peace and absorbs the tourists without disturbing the sounds of silence all around. There are picnic tables and wildflower trails and bird and wildlife preserves . . . nothing very jarring. Things would look pretty much the same except for the new inn erected in 1790, late around here, the

WASHINGTON CROSSING INN
Washington Crossing, Pennsylvania

BECALMED IN MID-VILLAGE, this is a classic white sprawl of an inn scalloped by some antique trees in front, the prototype of such places. Lovely. Dignified. The fire in the lobby leaps up as you enter and the logs give off a spicy smell. You are expected, yes, and it seems your table is waiting. The gold room with its yellow cloth, flowers, silver, burns off the memory of the gray, wan day outside. The service, ever-hovering in the wings, reminds anyone with a long memory of the dear dead days of Pullman-car dining. The menu is endearingly of the same vintage, a roll-call of long-standing Sunday traditions such as French lamb chops with mint jelly, roast duckling with wild rice, and, of course, roast prime ribs of beef.

Iced relishes, honorable staple of another time, arrive swiftly. Then a welcome new tradition, a loaf of hot bread delivered up steaming on a plank. It disappears at alarming speed, interrupted by excellent onion soup, by salad and at last by the entrée, a slab two fingers thick of rich rare prime ribs, the pride of the kitchen. Mountain brook trout *amandine* which was touted as fresh might have tasted better had someone frozen it en route to table from that brook; despite a topping of sliced almonds thick and overlapping as scales, it was not a success. Vegetables were familiarly overcooked, but were easy to ignore among the mountains of food. For dessert there are other classics from the past like baked Alaska flambé and old-fashioned strawberry shortcake though neither are available on Sunday. Dinner with drink and dessert will hover around $10.00. Lunch with soup, salad and the same ambiance, but without dessert, is lighter—around $2.50 and $3.00 for eggs Benedict, Cape May fresh fish or old-fashioned white-meat-only chicken salad. There's also an imaginative sandwich list.

There are several dining rooms upstairs and down, all charming in their fashion. To eat by the fire ask for the Hearth Room where the fireplace is big enough to set up housekeeping (it was, as it happens, the original kitchen).

The roomy guest rooms, while no museum settings, are welcoming enough, and have private baths and air conditioning. The new manager can't do much about the knotty pine panelling but he promises to whisk away the plastic flowers before you arrive. According to a long-time Bucks County watcher, the most time-honored tradition at Washington Crossing Inn is see-saw operation. Only history will decide whether the new regime wins this twentieth-century battle.

Washington Crossing Inn, *Rtes. 532 & 32, Washington Crossing, Pa. 18977. 9 mi. S of New Hope. Vero Bent, Prop. Open from 11.30-10.30 Tues.-Sat., 1-10 Sun. Closed Mon. & Christmas. AE, BA, DC, MC. Reservations a good idea weekends. Phone: 215-493-3634.*

UPCOUNTRY

FOR COLLECTORS of American landscapes there are few stretches as luxurious to the eye as the drive upriver from Washington Crossing or New Hope. Dreamy. Then melodramatic. Then dreamy again. Hardly a roadside stand or a signboard all the way to Easton. The DELAWARE CANAL in its parallel course with the river companionably appears and disappears at your side as the road strings together wild, eighteenth-century pastorals full of surging hills, rock upheavels, plummeting waterfalls and up near KINTNERSVILLE, five-hundred-foot-high palisades the Hudson valley might envy with simple, unmolested villages.

119

LUMBERVILLE, eight miles above New Hope, must be the prettiest of these. The village is lined with houses of stone or wood that have stared out at the water for centuries as if awaiting some magnificent regatta to sweep into view from around a bend upstream. It has one church, one post office, one antiques store, and three inns, two of which offer overnight accommodations. The most famous of these is a small hotel that started out 200 years ago — long before there was a canal hereabouts — as refuge for river travellers . . . these days is a refuge for the incurable romantic: it's the

---

BLACK BASS HOTEL
Lumberville, Pennsylvania

SINCE 1949 the Black Bass has been the undeclared National Trust of Herb Ward and, more recently, his factotum, Irene Stone, who walked across the footbridge from Raven Rock, New Jersey, one day, knocked on the door and started to work before she was hired. If the plaster has pulled off a bit here and there so you can see clear through to the fieldstone, why that's the way he wants it, she'll tell you. "He had a fit the time I got into the wine cellar and started dusting some of the bottles. He says he *likes* the dust on the bottles!" She shrugs as she snips away at the wild pink roses gathered that morning, determined to go along with the idiosyncracies of her boss. "This here is a *country* hotel," with a nod at the work-in-progress.

Upstairs on the second floor you'll find the guest rooms. All but two open onto balconies — step out and watch the silver-scaled Delaware go by in all its splendor as if it had been re-channeled to pass below your window, **there**, and stage all this watery spectacle for you and you alone. And inside another kind of splendor, of great Victorian carved beds covered with handmade antique quilts and marble-iced Victorian dressers. What if the bathroom is down the hall and shared with others? Small sacrifice, and there **are** washstands in the rooms.*

Downstairs in the little parlor, swaybacked Windsor chairs are drawn up in front of the fireplace for a bit of a chat and the cashier's desk like some pulpit stands over in one corner by the window where dozens of plants jostle each other for position.

Deeper inside are the dining rooms, large and small, and the flash of silver streaking through the windows is the Delaware itself.

In the summertime the place to eat is on the large screened veranda. As the river slides by just out of reach beyond the lacy iron balus-

---

*There is one suite available that sleeps four — complete with private bath and living room.

trade, lazy old ceiling fans paddle the air overhead; the feeling is like being on a riverboat down near New Orleans. Herb Ward submits Pennsylvania is where New Orleans **got** its trademark. The iron grillework that is identified with the French Quarter was made up north and shipped south. On a steamy day realists may prefer to descend below and join the wines cooling off in the wine cellar in airconditioned comfort. There are tables here and the river is even closer up.

Few kitchens could live up to such a setting and the Black Bass' isn't one of them. Here you eat Restaurant Roulette. Three chefs, one French, one Mexican, one Southern, take turns as head-of-staff, and the menu crosses French with southern cooking. The list is long and rarely boring: Peak's Island lobster bisque, strawberry soup, shrimp crêpes, brandied veal, roast duck Normandy and Charleston Meeting Street crabmeat, Pontchartrain ice cream pie, all calligraphed on brown parchment with the greatest elegance. If only one could eat menus! The vaunted wines are only vaguely described and prices are puffed. For the best odds, come here in the middle of the day; the menu is shorter, but the prices are lighter and disappointments come as mere pinpricks since lunch is just something that comes with the ride.

Rooms are $25 a night (single or double) including a continental breakfast waiting at your door in the morning. No extra charge if you eat it on the balcony.

Black Bass Hotel, *River Rd. (Rte. 32), Lumberville, Pa. 18933. Located 8 mi. upriver from New Hope. Herbert E. Ward, Prop. L—noon-2.30; D—5.30-10, Sun. 1-8. Closed Christmas Day.* Lodgings. DC, MC. *Phone: 215-297-5770.*

Two minutes away by raft, five on foot is the

1740 HOUSE
Lumberville, Pennsylvania

THIS IS SOMETHING like a private guest house where the host, kindly but remote, sees to your creature comforts before abandoning you to the seduction of your surroundings — the hypnotic glide of the river at your feet and the slow drip of time. Or perhaps a walk from nowhere to nowhere along the towpath that divides canal from river? Or a swim before breakfast in the jewel-like pool on the patio?

The best place to dissolve, to just be, is on the patio or balcony outside your room where the trees part enough to permit a view of the spangly early-morning-river or the streaming pewter road at night.

The 1740 House huddled down at the water's edge is a clutch of buildings, some new, some old. It's linked by sheltered brick walkways and at the core is a civilized sitting room with a fireplace that burns off the chill and the distance between strangers when it turns cool. There's a card room set up to go, too. This is what it has. What it hasn't are phones in the rooms, a single television set, a bar. You'll have to bring your own supplies; the kitchen is happy to refrigerate your wine.

The rooms are furnished in W. J. Sloane's best country house style: quilted flowery spreads, king-size beds, a genteel writing table, rattan chairs, several tôle lamps, a few discreet prints. Unseen technicians have adjusted the air conditioner for your arrival. Unseen hands turn down the blankets for you each night. No, this is *better* than being a guest in someone else's home. Here you are free to smile or frown, to read in the presence of others, or **not** to make a fourth in mixed doubles. You don't have to talk to a soul before breakfast, just a curt nod to those assembled on the terrace where a buffet breakfast is set up: orange juice, hot croissants or Danish, butter and jams, and coffee (freeze-dried, however). If desired, hardboiled eggs split and buttered in the Pennsylvania Dutch manner are available.

In season, dinner is served nightly Tuesday through Saturday to guests and occasional non-guests by reservation only. The unpredictable menu is limited to two or three choices from night to night. This night, a chilled avocado soup (no run-of-the-mill soup *de jour!*) or a fresh, sweet *pâté* that's not the usual over-unctuous paste. Then a filet of lemon sole *amandine* on a bed of crabmeat — quite good — served with macaroni *au gratin*, stewed tomatoes, salad, and home-baked bread. The wind-up is a brimming bowl of fresh strawberries snowed with whipped cream or the world's best devil's food cake with fudge icing *à la mode* and a worthy coffee.

If you're down for the weekend your host suggests "eating in" on Saturday night when most restaurants in the area come apart at the seams . . . a splendid suggestion.

> 1740 House, *River Rd., Lumberville, Pa. 18933. 6½ mi. N of New Hope on Rte. 32 (River Rd.). Harry Nessler, Prop. D at 7 & 7.30 by reservation only Tues.-Sat. Restaurant closed Sun. & Mon. (oftener in winter). Lodgings & light breakfast. Phone: 215-297-5661.*

It's not easy to forget some things and after twenty-eight years Amanda Colligan, one-time Dione Lucas student, can still stir up a fine omelette for lunch at the

CUTTALOSSA INN
Lumberville, Pennsylvania

... AND HER PURIST'S salad — oil and vinegar and lettuce leaves and a few cranks of pepper — is perfection. But this isn't why you come to the Cuttalossa. Nor is it the chicken *tettrazini* or the beef *Stroganoff* (which Dione would disown since it is prepared ahead, well-done rather than rare), nor the stuffed tomato salads, nor the b-l-t down. You go because it's the most romantic spot imaginable to have lunch on a summer's day, a shady table by a stream in full view of a fuming waterfall. Add a glass of chilled white wine or iced coffee: this, too, is soul food.

A cock bestrides the aisles between the tables looking for a handout or maybe for his old feathered friends murdered one by one by a sly neighborhood fox over the past winter. (*Here, fella — have some of this nice, stale roll while I eat the homemade banana bread.*)

You might come too for drinks on a Saturday evening. The crumbling stone grist mill across the footbridge where birds like to nest becomes an outdoor bar. Afterwards you might not be overly concerned that most of the offerings on the dinner menu could be turned out by any competent short-order cook. The entrées are bolstered by good soups and good desserts, mostly pies, made on the premises. In addition a carrot cake catered by one of the local talents is exceptional even in this carrot-cake country.

The inner inn has its charms too. If there are eight in your party you may reserve the private dining room which looks exactly like a private dining room in a private home *provided* the private home you have in mind is furnished with well-chosen eighteenth-century antiques – even to the high chair.

On a raw November night you could do worse than drop in downstairs. The room is small, seductive, with stone walls and stone floor and a fire to eat by. The table is set with panache – mile-high brass candlesticks, a pelican standing tall on the back of a turtle, said to be Chinese, part of the Colligan family collection. Those are genuine Windsor chairs. How charming it all is! But the hour is late. The cook is resting.

> Cuttalossa Inn, *River Rd. (Rte. 32), Lumberville, Pa. 18933. About 6 mi. N of New Hope. Amanda K. Colligan, Prop. L – noon-2.30; D – 5.30-9.30, Sat. 5.30-10. Closed Sunday, and Dec. thru March. Phone: 215-297-5082 or 297-8985.*

Instead of the canard about eating-where-the-truck drivers-eat follow the **chef** on his night off, or any knowledgeable innkeeper or restaurateur – the pro's. In this part of Bucks County they come running home to

---

PIPERSVILLE INN
Pipersville, Pennsylvania

THERE'S BEEN AN INN at this country crossroads since Revolutionary times and an innkeeper Brugger for the past fifty years. The present owner was literally to the manor born . . . in the room above the bar. The present structure was built in 1884 on the ashes of Piper's Tavern, a landmark during the early days of this country at the crossroads of a village that seems to be missing too. At one time or another Piper's Tavern with its stately columns was host to Ben Franklin and General Wayne, General Lafayette and Robert Morris, Bishop White and Joseph Buonoparte, who brought his own cook and silver – a goodlie companie. It pinch-hit then as an upcountry branch of the county seat of Newtown, In a sense it is still: the bar **is** the neighborhood. The walls are cluttered with paintings by patron-artists.

Though all during dinner fathers and mothers and strings of children and assorted relatives traipse into the half-timbered dining rooms with their heavily respectable old sideboards that have been polished to a dark gleam, later on—when the old folks and the young folks are safely in bed—they dance on the bars, according to a reliable source.

Be that as it may the food is not only honest but good, not only good but consistently good year after year. We like to think of food like this as home-style, but not too many homes can cook up a storm in a soup pot like the Pipersville' Czech chef. The beef-vegetable soup is a masterpiece no less, full of unexpected middle-European ingredients like dried mushrooms and barley and unexpected depths, while the bean soup is pungent and earthy. If you avoid the beef Wellington—a steak in a steam cabinet of bread dough—and stick to the standards, the steaks and the roasts and the duck, the well-seasoned vegetables served family style—"real food"—you'll fare exceedingly well. Even the lunches have heft. The Bruggers are German originally and there are the little reminders, like the weekly *sauerbraten*, the house shrimp in German beer batter, or a startling "liverwurst mitt onion" amid the turkey club's on the lunch menu. Browsing among the desserts, you'll find a superb New York cheesecake that could make a reputation for itself even in Cheesecake City and now and then, a homemade carrot cake. You won't have to import your own pastry chef as poor Joseph Buonoparte did in those good old days.

> Pipersville Inn, *Old Easton Rd., Pipersville, Pa. 18947.*
> *Located 9 mi. N of Doylestown at crossroads of Rtes. 611*
> *& 413. Joseph Brugger, Prop. L—noon-3; D—5-10, 1-8.30*
> *Sun. Closed Mon. MC. Phone: 215-766-8540.*

There is a large colony of accomplished amateur cooks along the banks of the Delaware. They create an atmosphere in which good restaurants flourish. In addition, every now and then, one of these local talents "goes public" and opens up a restaurant. Opens a restaurant as a child might set up a lemonade stand. There is always some ready-made, picturesque old place, a barge stop or abandoned tavern or rotting river hotel, for stage—a place to hang the sauce pots and the crepe pan and the copper bowls and the dripping spider plants and go to work. Uneven, occasionally exasperating, these amateur productions are still your best chance to find true happiness at table. But you'll have to be quick, before success spoils the sauce . . . before prices rise like soufflés . . . before everybody packs up and goes home. So grab a bottle of a good vintage and hurry over to

CARVERSVILLE INN
Carversville, Pennsylvania

ROBERT DACER of Toad Hall fame* is now operating on two burners, literally, in this half-forgotten Victorian hotel on the village square of old Carversville—a beautiful, remote corner of Bucks County. Décor is minimal, just some quick effects, shadow lanterns made with colanders and graters, but what a feeble thing is décor when the room, the building, the whole village looks like an abandoned movie set. In the rear a fitful fire draws the chill out of an early spring evening.

This man can make a filet dance to his tune better than anyone, anywhere, but it's showing off to limit three out of four entrées to steak. And number four—French-cut loin lamb chops in puff pastry—is fat as streak o' lean. The meal swings wildly back and forth from near-misses (an enormous but undercooked artichoke) to glorious (steak Enrico . . . a prime piece of beef expertly cooked and served on toast saturated in the intense Burgundy-and-shallot sauce), from yesterday's cold apple pie to a superb carrot cake. The coffee has greatness. Every little crumb, good or wide-of-the-mark, is à la carte, including the bread, the potatoes, the vegetable, the salad, and there's a charge of $1.00 for corkage, and, crumb by crumb, it adds up. Up to $12 or $13 per person (sans tip). *That* should help make up for the loss of bar profits, the financial underpinning of most restaurant operations, but it asks for something too.

A follow-up call reveals that there've been a lot of changes made since this visit, predictably enough. Note such beautiful Baroque appetizers as baked pear stuffed with Roquefort and blanketed in *mousseline* sauce or canteloupe piled with red caviar and sour cream —sheer verbal intrigues or a never-to-be-forgotten moment? Some of the steak items have made room for chicken velvet or clams oregano or Italian meat loaf or deviled shrimp. On a recent Saturday night, there were no steaks to be had at all! Vegetables, now that summer's arrived, swing with the offerings at local roadside stands. Where, this side of a Chinese restaurant, would you come upon a delicacy like snowpeas? Desserts too—French strawberry shortcake, peach cobbler, blueberry buckle reflect the pickings from nearby farms.

Even the schedule is different than before. They're now open Friday *through* Monday for dinner only.

Carversville Inn, *Fleecy Dale Rd., Carversville, Pa. Located about 4 mi. N/NE from Lahaska off Rte. 202 or 2 mi. W of Lumberville. Robert Dager, Prop. Schedule (subject*

*Defunct restaurant located at the site of Grace's Mansion.

to change) D only 7-10 Wed.-Sat., 1-5 Sun. in season. Call before coming, reservations a wise precaution: 215-297-5510.

An assistant to a theatrical producer and an advertising copywriter left all that behind when they bought this former, rather isolated barge stop and opened a restaurant *they* could eat at happily. Unlike other such ventures, this one has survived . . . gives every indication of carrying on till you get here. If you're barreling down River Road, however, it's easy to miss

---

THE GOLDEN PHEASANT
Erwinna, Pennsylvania

HUDDLED BETWEEN CANAL AND RIVER in an ambush of greenery, it's a brown hen of a golden pheasant from the road. Once past the shambly porch, however, you are in a hothouse of decorator Victoriana where the dark is thick as velvet and painted glass lamps glow like stains. If you're heliotropic you'll head at once for a table in the greenhouse where a lingering night descends in its own good time, little by little, and the many pinpointy lights inside come out unobtrusively as stars.

Since it *is* a glass house refrain from throwing stones when you are told, coolly, that the venison is, of course, unavailable this time of year and the featured namesake bird ("Pheasant of the Inn, Green Grape sauce") unavailable weeknights unless ordered ahead—*of course.* (Why this last piece of information is not imparted when reservations are made is unknown at time of writing.)

"You're going to think this is some kind of flim-flam house," said the waiter, "but we're completely out of half-bottles of anything." You pick a nice little $12 Montrachet, but there are worse fates. Gazpacho when it comes tastes like a Bloody Mary with a fistful of chopped greens but with the coming of *moules marinière*, a special of the evening, you are quickly mollified and the tossed salad, strewn with mushrooms is very pleasant. When the entrées come, all is forgiven: turbins of flounder upholstered with crabmeat in a sensuous lobster-sauce sea. Or the tenderest veal *piccata*, each round lightly coated with something like a fritter batter and flashed in the pan, the flavor quickened ever-so-subtly with lemon. Desserts did not meet expectations raised by this superb second act, but in more ordinary circumstances would pass muster. Strawberries *Romanoff* prepared in a chafing dish do in the ice cream they've spooned over which may be why the early fathers decreed this dish be made with whipped cream.

And the chocolate mousse is, well, resistable. A pot of espresso arrives wrapped in white napkin and presented like some rare wine, the treatment such great espresso deserves.

If you have overindulged and decide against serpentining home along the river why there is help at hand. Upstairs there are a trio of guest rooms in the favored Victorian style. But prepare to rough it. There's but a single communal bathroom and no reading lamps at all. Quoth the management: You're not *supposed* to read in bed.

Golden Pheasant Inn, *River Rd. (Rte. 32), Erwinna, Pa. 18920. Located 14 mi. N of New Hope on Rte. 32, 18 mi. W of Flemington via Rte. 12 and Rte. 32. Reid Perry & Ralph Schneider, Prop. D only—6-10.30, from 5.30 Sat., 4-10 Sun. Closed Mon. Lodgings. Reservations a must weekends: 215-294-9595 or 6902.*

NEWTOWN AND DOYLESTOWN

You CAN REACH NEWTOWN by Interstate 95, a speedy new four-lane testimony to the conquest of America by car. But it would be less of a cultural shock to come by way of Route 532 or some other back road that runs helter-skelter through the surviving country and leads you slowly back in time till you are deposited – gently – in the middle of the eighteenth century in the center of Newtown, Pennsylvania.

Somehow, Newtown has managed the miracle that we are likely to think of as European – of living simultaneously, unselfconsciously in both the present and the past. No groveling before ancestors, but at the same time no systematic demolition of all that's gone before such as takes place with bell-tolling regularity elsewhere. Time-honored old buildings are not torn down or frozen into museums, nor are they cannibalized as tourist shops. These are your pizza parlor, your five and dime, your bakery (said to be excellent), your cleaners. In the fine old houses life goes on; private homes still, they may be visited once a year during the annual pre-Christmas tour on the second Saturday in December. Old brick sidewalks, rolling as the high seas, still have right of way. One of them will lead you to the door of a neat little two-story building of gold-gray fieldstone with flag-red shutters called

129

TEMPERANCE HOUSE
Newtown, Pennsylvania

IN 1772 when the Temperance House was built it was no temperance house but a tavern and a schoolhouse in one. The owners, schoolteacher Andrew McMinn and bartender Nancy McMinn, man and wife, were duly recorded as "two good customers." In the saber-rattling of the history books it has somehow been forgotten how much history was actually written and business conducted, much like the three- and four-martini lunch of today, under the roofs of taverns and, let it be said, under the influence of strong spirits. Newtown was the county seat and according to the local signpainter, EDWARD HICKS,* "every tenth house was a tavern and every twentieth of bad report." A few decades later the Temperance House, repented and tee-totaled—thus the name.

Today the bar is still (or again) the heart of things, substantial, mellow, the gloom illuminated by the gleam of brass, the glitter of bottles, the glow of leather, and buzzing with bonhomie. The food has a good reputation locally and it should. It is good. Moreover it's cheap. The predictable lunch menu with its fried flounder and seafoods, its sandwiches hot and cold, is priced all the way from $1.00 to $2.25! Dinner specialties—duck with plum sauce, deviled clams, crabmeat imperial and a startling chicken salad with fried oysters—start at $3.00. An entrée of roast stuffed turkey served with two vegetables and a salad is $3.25.

There is a real live chef in the kitchen, Charles Richardson, a man of conscience with a hat two-feet tall who is not afraid to wrestle with real live turtles to bring you his superior brand of snapper soup. The chef, who left his last post at a well-known country club because management wanted to introduce flash-frozen, catered foods makes all his own soups and sauces from scratch.

His sacrifice is justified by the crabmeat imperial; the crabmeat may not be the fanciest or the lumpiest, but the preparation goes a long way toward masking the economics and the result is lovely eating. Alas, the famous plum sauce won't be available till evening, but the chef gallantly agrees to serve the duck that goes with it, a dinner hour specialty. Fortunately, the duck itself is delightful—moist inside and crunchy outside—and needs nothing. The rest of the meal involves creamed spinach, genuine mashed potatoes, a goodly salad

---

*You may remember Citizen Hicks as the artist who painted nearly 100 "Peaceable Kingdoms."

and a slab of uneventful apple pie, all pleasant enough if nothing for the history books.

If you're coming for the house tour, consider arriving the night before and staying upstairs in one of the two or three guest rooms. All are as clean and tile-bathed and neuter as any triple A motel, but all you need to do there is sleep which you should do well at the price: $11.00 for the single, $15.00 double.

> Temperance House, 5 S. State St., Newtown, Pa. 18940. Located off I-95, about 7 mi. SW of Washington Crossing. H. Clifton Neff, Jr., Prop. L — 11.30-3; D — 5.30-10 week-days, noon-9 Sun. Most cards honored. Bar, hot sandwiches and snacks till midnight or later. Lodgings. Phone: 215-968-3341.

Castles aren't a dime a dozen in America but in Doylestown, the bustly county seat of Bucks, there are *three*. All were built by one extraordinary man, Dr. HENRY MERCER, an eccentric or a genius or both. Dr. Mercer was a man in the Jeffersonian mold for which they have lost the formula today. Anthropologist, archeologist, historian, ceramicist, ecologist, horticulturist—and **rich**. Like Jefferson he became his own architect. Fifty years before anyone else he built with reinforced poured concrete and used the "crazy" construction techniques some of which have become today's orthodoxy.

The "Normandy" castle is the MERCER MUSEUM, designed as a showcase for his collection of Early Americana, a numbing 30,000 artifacts, many displayed as he directed out in the open, suspended in mid-air, and others arranged in rooms. It's open every day but Monday ten months a year (closed January and February) for a modest admission charge.

The second is the MORAVIAN POTTERY AND TILE WORKS resembling three famous California missions in one. *Dr. Mercer's* mission was to save for the world the moribund techniques of Pennsylvania-German pottery making. And he did—for another half-century. The tiles he has made are found throughout this part of the world as well as the Pennsylvania State Capitol building in Harrisburg and the gambling casino in Monte Carlo.

The third is FONTHILL, his home, a Gothic novel's idea of a castle, full of turrets, pinnacles, columns, arches, vaulted ceilings and eerie lighting effects. Everywhere it's encrusted with a magnificence of tiles—his own or his collections. For a small consideration, his former housekeeper is willing to hustle you through, up and down and under and around and out. Sometimes at breakneck speed. But worth it.

There is another man in this town as extraordinary in his way, a man with a sense of mission. You'll find him—and some of the best food to be had between New York and Philadelphia—at

CONTI'S CROSS KEYS INN
Doylestown, Pennsylvania

IF YOU TRIED to locate the Cross Keys Inn from the flattering self-portrait on the placemat you might be in trouble. Where are the trees, the softening shrubs, the leisurely canopied entrance? So much mulch now under the expanded parking lot. The inevitable expansion took place a few years ago leaving in its wake a well-behaved modern restaurant, with black leather banquettes and a scattershot of lights in the dimness.

But wait — walk around to the other side if you'd like a look at the old Cross Keys on the old Easton Road, the tidy white brick tavern with neat black trim, looking as it must have looked most of the two hundred years it has been in operation. Inn-collectors will want to eat in this — the original — part of the building. Gastronomes might be made happy by even a doggie bag at the door — *any* door.

Two generations of Conti's have operated this place and Walter Conti, a man possessed, trying to earn Michelin stars on American soil, is the moving spirit both behind scenes and out front. As he says: "When I'm greeting people, seating people, tossing salads, flaming dishes, I'm resting." Long before that you can find him in the kitchen, inspecting or rejecting, or trimming chicken breasts so that all are *exactly* the same size and none must sit around morosely in the pan waiting for the grosser pieces to cook up while their own flavor and juices seep away. Vegetables too must be diced *so*, and sauces reduced *so*. Between dessert and coffee, he runs out and teaches his fanatical views on food preparation and management to the Big Mac generation . . . like buying only the best and freshest . . . the fallacy of short-cuts and freezer foods . . . the importance of the finger in the pie . . . at a nearby college. He trains the staff personally, ten cooks and a chef. Even so, there are occasional lapses with so many cooks on so many burners. But all in all, he *has* succeeded in defying the law that says quality and finesse are found in inverse ratio to the number of choices (there are over seventy!) and the number of mouths to feed.

Knowing Conti is something of a status symbol locally, and fans look shocked when you suggest going somewhere else. Shocking you agree when you taste the fresh poached salmon rising like an island from a creamy pool of homemade tarragon-flavored caper sauce. Does it look a *bit* messy? Fiddle dee dee. It tastes like a soft, sensational coral cheese and the sauce is sublime. Or a bowl, an explosion, of navy-blue mussels, a ridiculous number of them (the waitress has to provide two empty platters just to cart off the shells), each one scrubbed till it glitters. The gold-and-green-flecked *sauce marinière* — though it could be a mite more concentrated—has good character. A California gourmand, himself surprised, can find no fault with the Caesar salad, mixed tableside. There are enormous dessert-lovers' desserts trundled about on a cart so you know what you're missing as well as what you're getting. Here's tall, interesting-looking chocolate rum cake . . . chocolate mousse . . . strawberry shortcake with real strawberries, real whipped cream made the *real* way with short short biscuit. And more.

The most old-fashioned thing about Cross Keys is the service. Waitresses (well-drilled) wait with interest while you make the most difficult decisions of your life, offer advice when courted, and return with all deliberate speed with the object all sublime. No one rushes you* . . . your table is your table for as long as you care to stay, a day, a week. A week!

> Conti Cross Keys Inn, *Rtes. 611 & 313, Doylestown, Pa. 18901. Located 1 mi. N of Doylestown between new and Old Easton Rds. Walter J. Conti, Prop. L — 11.30-3; D — 3-11 Mon.-Fri., 4-11 Sat. Closed Sun., Christmas, New Year's & Memorial Day, 2nd week in Aug. AE, DC, MC. Phone: 215-248-3539.*

*This statement like most other claims is inapplicable on Saturday night. Saturday night is only for emergencies, says Walter Conti, shaking his head.

X.

PENNSYLVANIA
DUTCH COUNTRY

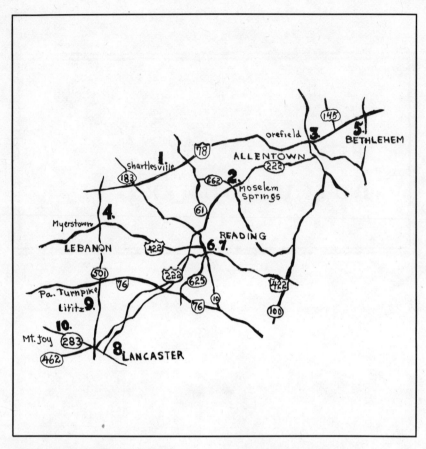

1. HAAG'S HOTEL
2. MOSELEM SPRINGS INN
3. LAUDENSLAGER'S
4. TULPEHOCKEN MANOR
   HOUSE
5. HOTEL BETHLEHEM

6. STOKESAY CASTLE
7. JOE'S
8. CENTRAL MARKET
9. GENERAL SUTTER INN
10. GROFF'S FARM

Transit companies serving the area: Bus from N.Y.C.—Transport of New Jersey (Myerstown, Bethlehem, Lancaster, Reading), Continental Trailways (Lancaster and Reading), Greyhound (Bethlehem, Lancaster), Martz Trailways (Bethlehem); Bus from Phila.—Capitol Trailways (Myerstown, Lancaster, Reading, Mt. Joy), Continental Trailways (Lancaster, Reading), Greyhound (Lancaster); Train from N.Y.C.—Penn-Central, Amtrak (Lancaster); Train from Phila.—Penn-Central, Amtrak (Lancaster), Reading Railroad (Bethlehem, Reading).

THE JOYS OF OVEREATING

AT ITS *best* Pennsylvania Dutch cooking is homely, down-on-the-farm cooking changing with the seasons and owing a heavy debt to the Old World (Dutch=*Deutsch* or German). The Pennsylvania Dutch are refreshingly insouciant about calories; as one consequence the seating in the recently built stadium in Reading is broader than anywhere else in the nation to accommodate the swollen crowds. The "7 sweets and 7 sours" that greet you from roadside signs are a traditional repertory of accompaniments among which you may find sweet-and-sour chow chow, sweet-sweet bread-and-butter pickles, pickled watermelon or canteloupe rind, pepper cabbage, cole slaw, corn relish, stewed apricots or peaches or rhubarb, apple sauce, applebutter, cottage cheese, pickled beets, cucumber salad, mustard beans, puddings, jellies, even cookies and cake. A few inches of bare table is an offense to the eye. Still game? Then let's go to

HAAG'S HOTEL
Shartlesville, Pennsylvania

CHARGE THIS MEAL to experience. A host of 20 or more satellite dishes accompany the main course which can be roast chicken ($4.00) or fried ham and chicken ($4.50) or roast beef, ham and chicken ($5.00). The glutton in you may leap up when you behold this bounty,

137

but the gourmet inside may have to pick and choose his way more carefully and, in the end, go hungry. You will probably like the pepper cabbage and the pot pie (not what you think, but big square noodles soused with chicken gravy); also the peas, the unctuous applebutter, the creamy cottage cheese, the rosy rhubarb sauce, an old-fashioned treat ladled over the tapoica pudding (these folks take their desserts as they come, i.e., before, during *and* after meals!). Best of all, big thick sugar cookies that taste, according to a fan, "like the first cookie you ever ate." But the chicken? Pale and uninteresting. The ham? The equal of the chicken, only saltier. And so on. Some of the side dishes, alas, come out of a can, and the bread is plain, flabby, wax-paper white. If you dote on pure glucose, you will find the pies, which like the cookies are offered for sale on a table as you come in, delectable. Their version of shoofly pie (a pie made with molasses) is pecan pie without pecans, so impacted it could give a diner lockjaw.

Shartlesville is a small village in farm country. Though tourists have been trooping through this region that lies just off new Route 78, you can dodge them by taking a back road in the direction of Bernville. Time reels backwards startlingly: you're in the landscape of childhood. The hotel, which is fieldstone with flower-stands like sentinels all around, is one of the last of a dying species and you should know about it, a true country hotel where—eureka!—a guest may pause for a night, a week, a summer. Though sixty-years-old, there's nothing seedy about it. The lobby like the porch outside is invitingly set up with mama and papa bear furniture—twiggy settees and chairs such as can still be seen in shady Adirondack cabins. The lobby shares space with a neighborly bar tended by the hotel manager, a Mr. Clemons. Good man.

The rooms upstairs are sweetly, cleanly old-fashioned with no attempt to hoke things up. Some have a washbasin ($6.00 single), some a shower; most share a toilet with another room. One relatively grand room with two double beds has the works, which will cost you all of $10.00. Breakfast, which we trust is more successful than the dinner is $1.50 to $2.50 for overnight guests only . . . if you're up to it.

> Haag's Hotel, *3rd & Main Sts., Shartlesville, Pa. 19554.*
> *Halfway between Allentown & Harrisburg on Old Rte. 22*
> *or I-78. Clemons & Clemons, Prop. Open daily from 11-7.*
> *Closed Christmas.* Lodgings *available. Phone: 215-488-*
> 6692.

Around July 4th, the "Gay Dutch"—to distinguish them from the "Plain People" whose capitol is Lancaster farther south—hold a festival in KUTZTOWN. Instead of a midway, craftsmen and craftswomen demonstrate the skills that reflect a way of life until very recently dismissed as extinct and now looked upon as the hope of the future, a whole-earth survival kit. For children, no Disneyworld productions, just covered wagon rides and buggy rides and when that palls, children's games. As you might expect there's lots to eat. Foods with funny names like pretzel soup and *fasnachts* (square doughnuts) and of course a variety of shoofly pies from the dry, dunkable ones to the wet, juicy ones. It's served in tents by the local women who throw in free cooking lessons. Did you think Pennsylvania Dutch hens laid those pickled eggs? Have you always wanted to make your own birch beer? Hurry on down.

Afterwards, if you can manage it, continue on course till you come to the

MOSELEM SPRINGS INN
Moselem Springs, Pennsylvania

THIS SLEEPY OLD BUILDING with the hitching post porch stood at these crossroads since 1852. From the road it looks a bit silly now with tourist trappings on the lawn, but inside it has dignity, even beauty. The foyer, furnished with antiques that are polished and shined like loving cups, looks like the entrance to a private, privileged house, and the dining rooms are tasteful.

The Moselem Springs Inn has a slew of admirers, and it does have a lot going for it, not the least of which are the prices. Dinners, complete, must be figured very close to the bone at $4.40 and $4.50 and $4.65 and all managing to stay under $5.00*.

If you have an inordinate craving for sweets and need a "fix" all through dinner as well as *after* dinner, you've come to the right place. Instead of 7 sweets and 7 sours they seem to have substituted 14 sweets, but who's counting? To keep you busy between courses, cinnamon crackers are served with a tub of lemon curd (like a sweetened butter) and this act is followed by a loaf of homebaked bread which is served with applebutter. Sweet-and-sour Dutch bacon dressing is sweeter than it is sour, corned beef is painted with apple-raisin sauce, and a side-dish of cottage cheese is stirred with cherries.

*Except steaks—no price is quoted.

Ah, but now that you've been warned you can easily skirt the problem. The minestrone soup served in an iron crock is packed with vegetables and pasta and pleasure. Pot roast, a generous serving, has a deep brown, deep-down flavor. The crowning glory, however, is the smokehouse sausage made right on the premises by Tommy Meyers, retired, from Allentown. Unbelievably good, bedded on potato filling and supported by horseradish and applefritters, it can hold its own among the world's great sausages. Available night or noon, you can also buy it by the foot or by the yard at the smokehouse store where they sell the corned beef, ham, bacon, and an excellent smoked chedder as well. Dessert — sheer anti-climax — is extra,* a tray of more interesting than usual pastries, but you give the nod to the beautiful, little fruit and cheese bowl and let it go at that.

> Moselem Springs Inn, *Rtes. 222 & 662, Moselem Springs,*
> *Pa. (Mailing address: RD 3, Box 10, Fleetwood, Pa. 19522.)*
> *Located 31 mi. N of Reading and 21 mi. S of Allentown.*
> *Madelyn & Walter Stoudt, Prop. L — 11.30-3 Mon.-Fri.,*
> *D — 3-10 Mon.-Thurs., 11.30-7 Sun. Note: Closed Fri. night*
> *& all day Sat., closed Christmas. Reservations Sundays*
> *& holidays: 215-944-8213.*

If you're stubborn . . . if you're sure there's more savor to Pennsylvania Dutch cooking than can be found at the big roadside feeding stations with their hex signs and their swollen claims (all you can eat for $3) and their tourist buses, your faith will be rewarded at

---

LAUDENSLAGER'S
Orefield, Pennsylvania

THE MENU, written in Early Restaurant English, gives no hint of anything much: roast young Tom turkey and t-bone steak and fried ham. No prime ribs — just roast beef. Not *soup de jour* but "soup of the day." Only the prices are extraordinary; unless you insist on steak or lobster, a complete dinner (relishes, soup or juice, potatoes, a vegetable and a salad, waffle, dessert and coffee) may be had for about six dollars; a hot lunch for $1.50-$2.00.

Laudenslager's is very popular, but it can't be due *entirely* to the prices; in an area where you're invited to shovel in all you can eat for $3 and $4, $6 ain't hay. Yes, it's the cooking. The Laudenslager's — man, wife and daughter — are in this together, and a waitress, indicat-

---

*Except ice cream and gelatin.

ing the hostess with her head, said in open admiration, "A better cook you're not likely to find."

You have to look closely at the menu to pick out localisms in the food. Fresh chunky country sausage, well-seasoned and juicy, and that staple in this part of the world, potato filling (honest mashed potatoes swirled with browned onions and parsley). A salad of pale green lamb's tongue lettuce in a hot creamy bacon dressing that's neither sweet nor sour but just right. Skip the stewed chicken, no star of this cuisine (it will remind the disadvantaged of home: pale and plain and probably very good for you).

Perhaps the kitchen is saving you for dessert: an old-fashioned apple dumpling, thoroughly delicious. The wrapper is half-cookie, half pie dough and the apple, even at this far end of the season, full of flavor. The runner-up, rhubarb-strawberry pie, is rewarding too, right down through the bottom crust.

We haven't mentioned the building for a reason. 1928 Georgian, it's full of pomp but little significance. Inside things are better. The decor is bric-y brac-y but the dining rooms are pleasant and comfortable with a luxurious sense of space between tables that we thought went out of style when the building was built.

Laudenslager's is just west of Allentown and very near the APPLE HILL SKI AREA and just north of some of America's most unspoiled countryside, the LEHIGH VALLEY.

> Laudenslager's Heritage Inn, *Rte. 309, Orefield, Pa. 18069. Located W of Allentown via Rte. 22 W to 309 N. The Laudenslager family, Prop. Open continuously 11.30-9 Tues.-Sat., 11.30-6.30 Sun. Closed Mon. & last 2 wks. of July. MC. Phone: 215-395-9995.*

Rarely do you find everything under one roof. Not too far away is a farm where they feed you like a spoiled child, all you want of all you want. Now, another kind of farm, a most unusual place, a retreat that offers just about everything else . . . but not a crumb to eat!

TULPEHOCKEN
MANOR HOUSE
Myerstown, Pennsylvania

THIS IS AN HONEST working farm with black Angus cows, sheep, horses, ducks, dogs. There's a cider house, a smoke house, a greenhouse, two spring houses, a fifteen-acre lake and a spring-fed brook. And you have the run of it—all 165 acres.

The manor house itself was built originally in 1730 by Capt. Michael Ley, Washington's good friend, from stone quarried on the farm. Later it was overlaid with all the familiar Victorian trappings — mansard roof, dormers, porches, carved wood balustrades and iron lace. The works. An awesome house. Inside the awe grows. The place is *jammed*. Floors are a patchwork of old Oriental rugs. Rare chandeliers of great beauty go unnoticed in the welter. Every foot of the way has its priceless piece — each is being lived with, sat upon, slept upon, or eaten from. **Used**. And there are 27 such rooms.

Beds are high and mighty Victorian fields of repose, fourposters or Empire, and covered in a magnificence of handmade quilts. There's a supporting cast of marble dressers, armoires, pier glass mirrors, tapestried footstools and ornate glass lamps. Tubs in adjoining or nearby bathrooms have claw feet. If you can sleep in a museum — for that is surely what this is (during the day tours are offered) — you are welcome to spend the night. But if you plan to stay a while you might prefer a modern apartment in a nearby spring house where you can cook. For food is not served here — to eat you must take to car or throw together a picnic. But sometimes there are more important things than eating . . .

Tulpehocken Manor House, *Rte. 422 (RD 2), Myerstown, Pa. 17067. Located between Reading and Lebanon, 2 mi. W of Myerstown. The Nissley family and James W. Henry, Prop. Lodgings only (single or double rooms or apts.) available all seasons. Breakfasts on occasion for overnight guests. Phone: 717-866-4926.*

PILGRIMAGE TO

BETHLEHEM

ONE OF THE EARLIEST communes in America was the Moravian settlement in Bethlehem. Life was lived, work performed and music offered up in the name of the church. The Moravians were master craftspeople and fanatically industrious. Their gravely beautiful Germanic-Moravian buildings of cut stone and hewed timber still climb the hill in the middle of town. Restored, yes. A restoration, no. They have grown used to Bethlehem and Bethlehem, them.

Down by Monocacy creek behind the main hotel in town, the remarkable pre-Revolutionary industrial center that Ben Franklin and George Washington came to study and admire is being put back together by a group of citizens and archeologists from on-site remains. It includes a sophisticated waterworks that served the entire community, a Plymouth Rock of American technology. There are guided and unguided walking tours available and a well-laid out riding tour.

The musical tradition runs deep, marked by the two-day BACH CHOIR FESTIVAL each year in the spring. Tickets—hard to come by—may be ordered from Lehigh University. But you don't need tickets to hear the famous trombone choir that announces all festivities—*and deaths*—from the belfry of the church and, in the dark before the dawn of Easter, stands at first one street corner then another, twenty trombones strong, pushing back the night.

If you'd like to hear them or to see the famous Christmas candles burning bright in every window in the old town which was founded this night in 1741, the place to be is the site of the old Eagle Hotel and the present

144

HOTEL BETHLEHEM
Bethlehem, Pennsylvania

"WE'RE ONLY a small country hotel but we try."

A small country hotel with the largest selection of wines in all Pennsylvania, from the poor man's Mateus, the Portuguese rosé, Alianca ($4), to a Chateau Mouton Rothschild '61 ($65). A small country hotel with *two* king-size beds and *two* baths to a room . . . with instant room service provided by a machine referred to familiarly as "the bell captain" (a turn of the key and it hands up a coke or something a good deal stronger made as you like it, with or without. Before you've had your first sip, the "captain" simultaneously signs for you downstairs at the desk. *Spooky*).

This inn that Bethlehem Steel money helped build in the young Twenties for its friends masks its luxe behind an undistinguished facade such as can be found genteely going to seed in hundreds of middling-size cities. Traditionally, entrenched money likes to hide its undulgences behind a mousey exterior, content to ride in a modest black Chrysler—even a Ford—and to huddle inside a raincoat from Abercrombie's. Mink is for linings. Let the *arrivistes* drive the flashy foreign cars . . . wear the diamond stickpins.

Of late, however, the Hotel Bethlehem, modeling itself on the Hotel du Pont in Wilmington, has more and more thrown off the trappings of the shabby rich. If the architecture is less than palatial, the appointments, the food, the furnishings are fit for a king—and, of course, captains of the steel industry. A marching band could slip through the aisles between the tables in the main dining room and the ceiling is hidden behind clouds. Expensive space for expensive people. The new green-banded bone china service plates are designed to order and cost $18.50 each . . . the long-stemmed cut crystal goblets, $7.50. (The polite rip-off, an estimated $500,000 business, hasn't reached this fortunate enclave.) Drinks are unusually expansive and well-made. The food when it comes is also 14-carat. The usual cast of relishes jeweled with ice. Elegant salt sticks and a baton of good French bread, bundled to keep warm. For appetizer, a freshly-made lovely crab meat *en chemise* (wrapped in a crepe then masked in béchamel sauce) . . . delicate prosciutto draped over—oops—not-quite-ripe melon. The salad, spinach bestrewn with Irish bacon, is superb. At the touch of a fork, chicken Kiev gushes forth the damned-up herb butter and bastes itself with it. The meat, macerated till it seems almost fluffy, is held together only by a thin skin of crumbs. Medallions of beef à la Stanley (filet, sauced with horseradish and cream and crowned with fried bananas) makes more interesting reading than eating; the filet, like so many filets, is a bit flat. Vegetables are offbeat: a green pepper stew or peas with apple, and a good version of potato filling, the Pennsylvania Dutch classic found as frequently as french fries elsewhere. Desserts lean heavily on ice cream but there's also a flambé'd *baba* or *crêpes Suzette*, or hot apple pie with brandy sauce.

It is not cheap, going first class. But it's *worth* it.

The informal Pioneer Room is open for both lunch and dinner and offers an occasional folk dish like *hoppelpoppel* (eggs with bacon, onions, potatoes *garni* and fried tomatoes, $2.00) and Moravian sugar cake. It seems even in this sophisticated outpost we are still in the land of the Pennsylvania Dutch.

> Hotel Bethlehem, *437 Main St., Bethlehem, Pa. 18018. Located in the heart of the historic area (take Center City exit off Rte. 378 . . . follow historic area signs). Frank T. O'Keefe, Prop. The Pioneer Room is open almost continuously from 11-10 Mon.-Sat. The Continental Room open for breakfast & dinner (6-10 Wed. & Thurs., till 11 Fri. & Sat., 1-10 Sun. Closed Mon. & Tues., also July & Aug. Lodgings. AE, BA, DC, MC, CB. Reservations a must weekends: 215-867-3711.*

SHOPPERS FROM PHILADELPHIA come up for the day claiming that it's easier to park in Reading than in downtown Philadelphia. Reading is the self-proclaimed discount center of America. There are guide lists available, coded, but most women won't need a code to decipher "David Crystal" or "Letisse" or "Vanity Fair" or "Carter," though they may need a map to run them down. Vanity Fair is actually in Wyomissing, just west of Reading, in a community of vintage red brick factory buildings, set down in a gracious park. Local historians will tell you that Reading was the hub of the silk stocking industry in the days when you could tell a lady by her stocking seams. The best one-stop house is said to be Cousins, but bargains as we know, are in the eye of the beholder.

Afterwards, sated, you may be more than ready to have lunch in a line-for-line copy of a twelfth-century castle that sits on top of the world:

STOKESAY CASTLE
Reading, Pennsylvania

IT WAS BUILT as a private home in the middle of the Great Depression after the original in Shropshire, England. Local materials were used and the result is lordly to say the least. "You don't go there for the *food*," a local critic protested, a bit embarrassed at the idea. What

147

then? There's the view. It unfolds for mile after mile till it reaches the very foothills of the Blue Mountains. For a ringside seat when the weather warms up, eat out on the patio. In winter gravitate to the fire in the Great Hall or the more intimate, wainscoted library.

The Caesar salad, which has been assembled somewhere offstage, comes as a shock of pleasure, defying criticism and critics. A sampler of desserts including a heady grasshopper pie, a crunchy pecan pie and a seductive cheesecake are each singularly fine examples of the species; an unknown artist comes in every day to do the baking. But there is no chef at Stokesay. No prima donna to undepend on. Instead, undemanding dishes prepared the "house" way by it doesn't matter whom—a good executive. The dinner menu is strewn with mystery dishes such as Pork David and Oysters Irwin as well as standards like calves' liver and lobster tails and steak Diane (never on Saturdays) and a lack of lamb ($9.95 for two). A la carte prices start at $4.50 and climb speedily to the $6 and $7 level. Relishes, potato and vegetable, and the view are thrown in.

> Stokesay Castle, *Hill Rd. & Spook Lane, Reading, Pa. 19606. Located just off Rte. 422. J. Phillip Hoeffer, Prop. L—noon-5, D—5-10, till 11 Sat., noon-9 Sun. Open daily year-round. AE, BA, DC, MC, CB. Phone: 215-375-4588.*

If Pottsville is O'Hara country and Shillington is Updyke country, then certainly Seventh and Laurel in downtown Reading is Updyke inner-city. Surely you remember where Rabbit Angstrom (*Rabbit Run, Rabbit Redux*) spent those early golden years of his coming of age? The neighborhood wasn't chi-chi then—it isn't the right side of the tracks now. Nonetheless it's where you'll find the gourmet shrine known as

---

JOE'S

Reading, Pennsylvania

IT IS AMONG these streets, among these red brick rowhouses with their art-deco glass panels above the doors, their stoop population curious-eyeing the stranger, across from a sudden small but dazzling Baroque church that seems to have been transplanted to this spot intact from the Old World. Joe and Wanda Czernicki are mycologists extraordinary. For two months a year they go on the hunt. The other ten they're back at this fine old address where a tavern has stood for over 150 years, where Joe's was born in 1916, doling out their bounty as if it were black gold. And charging for it. (It is doubtful with drinks going for $2.00 that the fellows in the neighborhood do much tanking up here anymore.) Still, wild mushroom restaurants don't grow like—mushrooms. In view of the scarcity be prepared to overdo it, and to pay for it.

First, wild mushroom *piroshkis* . . . three tiny pockets of exquisite pastry though all three together would not yield a whole chanterelle. Look further, hungrily. The wild mushroom soup, a dark brown brew thickened with sour cream, endorsed by Joe, who should know, is quite good but *still not the Holy Grail*. Veal Rymanow, two thinly pounded scallops of veal sandwiched with a thin layer of a wild mushroom and truffle duxelles, dipped in crumbs and sautéed, seems to be holding back, like so much else this night.

It isn't until you meet with a lovely little tart gorged with wild mushrooms in a creamy essence-of-mushroom sauce that you know what you came this far from home to find. It accompanies, with no special fanfare, the tenderloin *en brochette* or may be ordered à la carte at $1.50, the best bargain in all Reading. Four or more of these, chased by cold, thrilling beer would be worth the trip from **wherever** you are.

The side dishes are an oven-roasted potato and Belgian canned carrots (which taste no better here than they do anywhere else) and a lightly, perfectly dressed salad of Boston lettuce. Dessert is a peach tart. Somebody in the kitchen has the touch it takes for pastry — feathery — and the peach is cold and luscious, helped along with whipped cream **and** ice cream. Then an elegant espresso to put the period to things.

If you plan on coming, make it on a Friday or Saturday during the month of May for veal with fresh morels. It's a gamble. Still, if you are worthy of fresh morels, fresh morels are worth the risk.

> *Joe's, 450 S. Seventh St., Reading, Pa. 19602. Located in downtown Reading at corner of Laurel & Seventh. D only 5–9, Sat. from 4.30. Closed Sun. & Mon., also mushroom-hunting months of August & September. AE, BA. Reservations a must: 215-373-6794.*

LANCASTER, LITITZ

AND THE

PLAIN PEOPLE

ROUGHLY SPEAKING the Pennsylvania Turnpike is the Great Divide between the Plain People to the south and the Gay Dutch to the north. The Gay Dutch drive cars which they cautiously paint black to ward off the devil, a fellow who likes flash; their women doff their bonnets and men their beards, their children are permitted to go through high school. Amish who leave the church are said to "go Gay" and in one way or another they *are* beginning to leave. Moving west due to the high cost of farm land they, themselves, helped make fruitful through their skills, for the AMISH practiced sound ecology all along and taught the rest of us when we would listen. Moving away, too, from the incursions of tourists, who park and peer and poke cameras at them and tempt their children; sons of Amish farmers can be seen riding up behind the firehouses in their black buggies and sober clothes, speeding off in T-shirt and jeans behind the wheel of a car. Interbreeding among the 22,000 members of the Old Order Amish is taking a toll, too, in dwarfism, eye problems and "attic cases."

Still, to see a man walking through a field in the wake of a plow . . . to look upon little girls in poke bonnets and puffy skirts blowing like dandelion fluff across the lawn . . . makes a visitor homesick for a way of life at once more familiar than the palm of the hand and foreign as Yemen or the Yangste.

On a Tuesday or Friday morning there's no better place to be than the CENTRAL MARKET in Lancaster. The Amish come in with their worldly goods: bunches of radishes and scallions and baby asparagus beautiful enough to be brides' bouquets; spinach so fresh every leaf can teeter on end; a treasury of pickles and preserves put up at home; pot cheeses; cup cheese; apple butter and pear butter and just plain butter fresh from the butter churn; home-baked spankable breads; pound cakes and sponge cakes and yeasty doughnuts; fat, backyard chickens, home-smoked meats and sausages. Even flowers and plants. Come – and bring a big basket.

Historic-house collectors will find a town-within-a-town in LANCASTER well worth a walking tour. (The Central Market itself, built in 1889, is on the site of a tradition that goes back 230 years, and some of the stands have been staked out by the same family for generations.) Arm yourself with a guide (*Historic Heart of Lancaster*, by Gerald S. Lestz, available locally, $1.00).

If you plan to lay over, point the car north on Route 501 till you come to the

GENERAL SUTTER INN
Lititz, Pennsylvania

LITITZ (li titz') is another community that has aged well, but it's much smaller than Lancaster — cozier. Thanks to a nearby factory, the whole town is haunted by the smell of melting chocolate — dee-licious.

You can tick off eighteenth-century dwellings as you walk down Main Street till you finally reach the *pièce de résistance* — the pretzel factory. Visitors are invited to watch the twists and turns of pretzel making, now, alas, cranked out by soulless machines, and may help themselves to the broken ruins. Better though to save yourself for a fine old Pennsylvania Dutch treat, pretzels and ice cream available at the Pretzel House Restaurant adjoining the factory. If you're hungrier than that, there are local specialties like corn fritters with ham or bacon, or chicken and waffles, or a Dutch ham sandwich spread with — listen — "peach butter and golden mustard."

Lunch — or lemonade or something stronger — is also served on the tree-roofed terrace of the General Sutter Inn that overlooks whatever action there is on the main square. Traffic noise gets tangled in the trees and seems remote and maybe that's why everything tastes so much better than expected. If the fine pea soup and the savory stuffed cabbage rolls (made with whole, krauted cabbage leaves) are any indication, the new owner is a man of much promise. The hefty country salad bowl, bolstered with turkey and ham and roast beef and cheese strips, is another good way to go. The dinner menu lists lots of gimmicks but the small print reveals some items of more than usual interest: smoked baby spareribs or puffed jumbo shrimp in a fruit and mustard sauce. Soup, served from your own private kettle, is a specialty, and a help-yourself salad. Time will tell what the dessert policy will be. Prices are the usual Pennsylvania Dutch bargains: $6.95 for steak *on down* with most (complete) dinners staying under $5.00.

The hotel itself which we're told has been here in one shape or another since 1764, is soft red brick, exceedingly comfortable and a bit fuddy-duddy. Backward enough to provide a lobby for its guests. Patriotic enough to install first class plumbing for all the 14 rooms, along with TV and air conditioning. Rarest of all, good thick towels in the adult size. The housekeeper, who occupies one of the best rooms in the house, is a wiry woman of eighty-five who has worked all her life "with the Lord's help" and is living proof of His miracles.

> General Sutter Inn, *14 E. Main St., Lititz, Pa. 17543. Located 6 mi. N of Lancaster on Rte. 501. James J. Constantine, Prop. Open daily. L—11-2.30, D—5-10, till 11 Sat., from 11-8 Sun.* Lodgings & breakfast. AE, BA, MC. *Phone: 717-626-2115.*

There are times when the thin, self-protective show-me sneer of a restaurant critic doesn't work. As you reach for it, it comes unhinged and like some false moustache responds weakly or not at all. There you go over the rainbow into the country of childhood, a tourist among tourists. It's the risk you run if you spin off some green evening in May to

---

GROFF'S FARM

Mt. Joy, Pennsylvania

MAKE NO MISTAKE about it, this is a working farm among other working farms—Betty and Abe Groff's place. The yellow fieldstone house sits where it's sat for over two hundred years looking down on a pond cupped in a few quick hills. Some Herefords are posted randomly about, and one of their number is moving off ineluctably down a long valley that trails like a scarf behind the pond.

Inside, in all the rooms, the furniture (Victorian, pretty) has been pushed to the wall and tables improvised. Every able-bodied chair in the county must be here tonight! Waitresses in deep concentration come and go planting bowls of sweets and sours, then, returning and counting, make off once more to get a missing item or to snatch up a pot of African violets from a window reveal to use as a centerpiece. There's going to be a party for sure! A last pass through and the candles are lit, a sign to be seated, to begin.

Before you is a pride of relishes: an ever-so-subtly sweet-and-sour chow chow ... spiced Persian melon with a mysterious tingle ... sweet dark green pickle chips ... cloudy green cole slaw. Also cottage cheese and apple-butter and homemade bread and home-churned butter. Also cracker pudding, a rather fascinating side dish meant to be eaten before, along with, and in between courses like a palate cleanser (to tell you that it's made of eggs, milk, sugar, coconut, and thickened with crackers is to leave you knowing less than before). All are glories of the Groff kitchen as is the—blink!—chocolate cake still warm from the oven; it's crowned with white icing and cut into tall, crumbly squares. How's that for starters? (Anyone still worried whether salad should be served before or after the entrée or pie should be eaten at breakfast—things like that—will please leave the room.) The moral of the chocolate cake seems to be that a lot of people spoil their appetite for dessert by eating too much dinner first.

The waitress announces the first course: chicken soup with rice or fruit shrub. That out of the way we move on to more important matters—the dish Betty Groff named, arbitrarily, chicken Stoltzfus, that has helped bring everyone from Craig Claiborne and James Beard to governors and foreign dignitaries to her door. Morsels of chicken and little rafts of a remarkably flaky pastry in a saffron-gilded sauce. This, with a simply prepared slab of home-cured ham creates a chord that would be hard to improve on in any cuisine in the world unless you follow swiftly with a bite of the spicy melon. Shoring up these offerings are mashed potatoes swirled with browned butter and backyard asparagus dressed in more butter (a better sauce for fresh, fine raw materials has yet to be invented) and a bowl of home-canned tomatoes innocent of anything except a handful of tiny, invisible croutons that go crunch in the dark.

Betty Groff, a Mennonite farmer's daughter and wife, moves from table to table throughout the dinner, slim and pretty and sure of herself in an ankle-length *Town and Country* farmer's daughter dress. Only her hands give her away, two small but competent-looking shovels, a pastry cook's hands: she bakes every bit of the pastry herself. Tonight there's strawberry pie, strawberry cake or strawberry sundae, and ice cream this and that. And would you like ice cream with your pie? The pie, which *needs* nothing, is the same remarkable pastry encountered earlier but now bearing fresh glazed strawberries and muffled in whipped cream. The ice cream, homemade vanilla, is the ice cream waiting for ice cream lovers at the end of the rainbow or on Pinkerton Road.

Your hostess has few secrets from the world: "I'm going to have to spend next week canning," she says, shaking her head incredulously. "We're running out of everything." . . . "Did you see the new addition to the house? Abe and I are going to finish the inside ourselves but I don't see how we can have it done by June." . . . "No, we're closed Sunday and Monday. I'm going up to Rockport to work on a cookbook with my collaborator." . . . "When do I study speedreading? Oh, a few hours in the afternoon. I lock myself in my room—" She pots, too, Betty Groff. The ironstone with the wheat pattern you've been eating off of is not an heirloom but as homemade as the pickles; the kiln is in the laundry room.

The piano player is late—no, he's here. Dragging a young lad whom she's cajoled into playing drums, she moves off into the next room and raises her trumpet. Behold this! In a few minutes—without benefit of alcohol or anything except bonhomie—everyone is singing, all eighty guests including the Governor and his party. The drummer looking neither left nor right but straight ahead plays as if the drum were made of eggshells or even pie crust.

When you see her again you ask: "And what do you do with your feet, Betty-O?" "I make wine," she replies happily. "I make wine with my feet."

Then this Mennonite woman takes the guests, in trickles and streams, down to the winecellar where the dandelion wine is still going pop pop in its cask and gives everyone a taste of one of her homemade wines—cherry tonight. She also makes sixteen other varieties of folk wine including rhubarb and elderberry and locust blossom and strawberry and rose-petal and end-of-the-day wine.

Something seems to be missing and it's the check. No check is ever presented here and it's up to you to find affable Abe Groff. The fee is a uniform $6.50 whether you order the chicken with ham, with roast beef or with all three, whether you've had one or seven helpings. Reservations are essential. Wednesday, pot luck night, for the benefit of frequent returnees, is $8. If you glance into the darkened room where you have just fared so well you're in for a shock. Dishes, napkins, candles, silver, cloth, chairs, table—all gone, and there is a proper Victorian parlor waiting in the shadows.

Groff's Farm, *Pinkerton Rd., Mt. Joy, Pa. 17552. Located about 9 mi. W of Lancaster. Abe & Betty Groff, Prop. L seating—12.30. D seating—5 and 7. Closed Sun. & Mon. By reservation only: 717-653-1520.*

XI.

CHESTER COUNTY
AND BEYOND

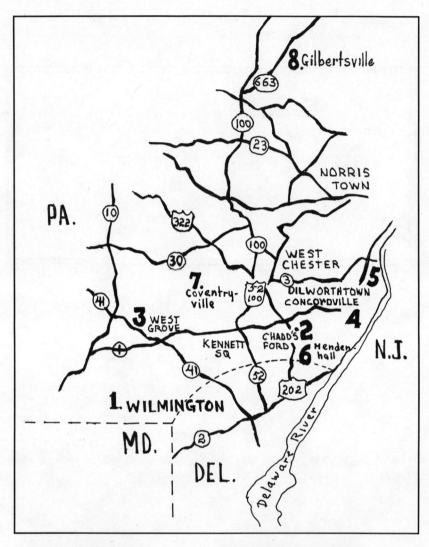

1. **HOTEL DU PONT**
2. **CHADD'S FORD INN**
3. **RED ROSE INN**
4. **THE OLD MILL**
5. **DILWORTHTOWN INN**
6. **MENDENHALL INN**
7. **COVENTRY FORGE INN**
8. **FAGLEYSVILLE COUNTRY HOTEL**

Transit companies serving the area: Bus from N.Y.C.—Continental Trailways, Greyhound, Martz Trailways (Wilmington); Bus from Phila.—Continental Trailways (West Grove, Wilmington, Concordville); Train from N.Y.C. *or* Phila.—Penn-Central, Amtrak.

A TASTE OF MONEY

THE EATING ALONG ROUTE 100 is probably better than can be had anywhere else in Chester county . . . problem with it is there are no restaurants. The people who live along this road are not like you and me, as Scott once said, since they are rich. *Very* rich. They eat at each other's table when they eat "out." But the country is beautiful and free if you don't try picnicking by the side of the road! You may drive all the way from Wilmington to Chadd's Ford, Chadd's Ford to West Chester on Route 100 and never see a twig bent in a discordant way. These are the private preserves of country gentry, people who live **on** but not **off** the fat green lush land that lies along the Brandywine. Their horses, when not summoned to the hunt or to the polo matches at Toughkenamon, graze indolently in the fields . . . their cows sit sidesaddle on the downy meadowgrass and their bulls win ribbons and spawn new dynasties. (King Ranch of Texas has a *pied à terre* not too far away, the BUCK AND DOE RUN FARMS near Coatesville, where their Texas-bred Santa Gertrudis cattle meekly munch and mark time.)

You've been here before. Wyeth after Wyeth, not to mention Wyeth sons-in-law Hurd and Weymouth and McCoy — it's a kind of cottage industry — have exactingly recorded with their paints and brushes every blade of grass and every ripple along the once-bloody Brandywine, the trees and the stone barns and houses that took root here two and three centuries back. Scenes as American as our vaunted apple pie and perhaps as elusive. (Graffiti artists have been busy too: Power to the people says the fist on the overhead railroad pass.) This portrait of a place and record of "the family" — the so-called Brandywine Sunday and Monday. I'm going up to Rockport to work on a cookbook with my collaborator." . . . "When do I study speedreading? Oh, a few

art school—can be seen at the beautiful BRANDYWINE ART MUSEUM on Route 1 near Chadd's Ford, an old, converted grist mill of brick and glass that bellies out over the water. For walkers and Sunday painters there's a path that starts here and trails upriver for about a mile.

This country, so gentle and pleasing to the eye, is metaphorically speaking very incestuous. In addition to the Wyeths there are the DuPonts. As you have doubtless heard, they've done very well here with their chemicals, and their tribe, too, has, indubitably, multiplied. They hold sway in Delaware (just down the road) where their name appears in connection with everything from the UNIVERSITY OF DELAWARE to WINTERTHUR* across the street, Winterthur to the hospital, the hospital to the DELAWARE RACEWAY and another legacy back in Chester County, LONGWOOD GARDENS.**

In Wilmington itself they have put their imprint on one of the last Quattrocento palaces built in this country (1913), maybe in the world—

HOTEL duPONT
Wilmington, Delaware

THE DU PONTS, as one reporter put it, do things *right*. When business associates come down—men of substance not used to hacking it at Sleepy Hollow motels with their formica dressers and paper-taped toilets and towels the size of washcloths—one has to put them up properly. In a city like Wilmington it left them no choice but to build. The order went out to spare no expense, and no expense was spared. What will it be? Polychrome-coffered ceilings three-and-a-half stories high? Travertine marble halls and roseal marble stairs? Golden chandeliers from Spain weighing, each one, 2500 pounds. To decorate the ballroom 30 artisans were brought over from Italy for two years, working in the now defunct medium called *sgraffito*. If you see an occasional Hepplewhite sideboard or Duncan Phyfe table or Philadelphia Chippendale chairs by the dozen, if you run into an eighteenth-century clock that shows the movements of the planets, or a Queen Anne highboy, don't dismiss them as reproductions. The Christina room, favored by the people who know these things, wears a million dollars worth of Wyeth's on its dark rich-panelled walls.

*Winterthur is a look inside America—100 period rooms full of American furnishings. It can be once-over-lightly in an hour or more extensive visits can be arranged by appointment. Admission is charged.

**Longwood Gardens, the end of the trail for admirers of formal gardens, may be visited year round as three and a half acres are under glass. Free.

A private club? Not at all. Quite frankly The Company needs the
rest of us to help keep their guesthouse going, and in these rough
times we could all use a few lessons in how things are done when
they're done *well*. Every Sunday for a pittance of $4.75 — little more
than the laundry bill for all that deep yellow double damask used with
Gatsby-like abandon — the townsfolk of Wilmington and the surrounding countryside, and of Philadelphia and Baltimore as well, descend

on the Green Room for a buffet breakfast. Under windows that rush up for two stories and chandeliers of gold leaf that explode in a blaze of glory overhead, a buffet is set up announced by a magnificence of field flowers arranged bloom for bloom after some Flemish still-life. Soaring above all is a brooding eagle hand-carved out of ice (another week you might find the Mermaid of Copenhagen or a fighting tuna). All this for us? Shall we clap? Is it done? White-capped chefs stand at the ready by their chafing dishes to whip up eggs, to pour the pancakes, plain or blueberry. There are sausages, bacon, roast beef hash, chicken à la king, panned potatoes, fruit salads, green salad, gelatin salad, sliced tomatoes, Danish pastry, petit fours and rum cake Napoleons—everything in excess. But a gelatin mold in this hallowed place? French pastry at *this* time of day?

"This is *not* a gourmet meal," said a haughty official, reprovingly.

What is it then? It's a party, that's what. Remember Charlotte Russe? Remember ambrosia? Remember chicken à la king and pineapple delight? All those old-fashioned party foods that belong to another generation?

As you return from the first trip, coffee awaits in sterling silver eminence on the table . . . also cut crystal bowls of sweating sweet butter, of amber guava jelly. And breads: a heap of hot biscuits and sweet rolls on a silver tray. When you return from the second trip with a row of made-to-order blueberry pancakes, a silver pitcher of pure maple syrup has materialized, at some unseen signal.

What if all you want is a soft-boiled egg?

The chef nods in the direction of a vanishing waitress sealed in an Edwardian black and white uniform. "She will bring you one," he said, surprised that anyone should ask.

Thursday night there's a buffet dinner ($9.75), an institution that has been going strong for 45 years. How bad can it be with a hotel that combs the world for the best raw materials, whose chickens are fed milk, whose beef is raised on corn, who regularly sends an agent to Maryland shore suppliers to instruct them in the proper way to remove crabmeat (in lumps—not shredded—and free of annoying bits of shell)? According to a knowledgeable spectator, the du Pont, after some lean years, has acquired a quite good chef. That should help even more.

This is one inn where the weary traveler is welcome to drink, eat, be merry and to rest! And in the morning, breakfast is served, in bed if you like it that way.

Hotel Du Pont, *11th & Market Sts., Wilmington, Del. 19899. H. V. Ayres, Gen. Mgr. Several dining rooms. Open year-round, for breakfast, lunch, dinner, snacks.* Lodgings. *AE, BA, MC. Reservations: 302-656-8121 or 8181 . . . Ext. 3156.*

WYETH'S WORLD

AFTER GOING THE ROUNDS of the local inns anyone might conclude that stuffed oysters and grasshopper pie are indigenous foods, like the mushrooms of Kennett Square. The oysters and the pie turn up on menu after menu with the frequency of classics such as cheesecake or onion soup. The explanation can be found by tracing the trajectories of one of two popular chefs in the area: their restless tours of duty from inn to inn and back again have left its mark on the eating habits of the natives. As these fellows flit about they take with them a moveable feast of hallowed recipes, their own plus a few *pièces de resistance* from the previous establishment. No one seems to mind. One innkeeper confesses openly and gleefully to pirating the original grasshopper pie recipe in the first place from a sister-in-law who had been supplying the improbable green pie and charging dearly for it. The free enterprise system at work.

Our cook's tour of the neighborhood includes a baker's half-dozen places that can be found within a few miles of each other up and down — and occasionally a few miles off — the old Baltimore Pike, the fabled King's Highway of pre-Revolutionary days. (You can also find it on your map as U.S. 1 but this largely rural stretch of America's main drag bears so little resemblance to the public image of Gasoline Alley it hardly seems fair.) Within a cannon shot of the BRANDYWINE BATTLEFIELD there's a weathered old inn of darkest stone, wrapped in a porch and memories that go back before 1736, when John Chad turned his father's house into a tavern

163

CHADD'S FORD INN
Chadd's Ford, Pa.

ENTER – and feel at once the spirit of place. Small dining rooms with their low ceilings and exposed floorboards look conspiratorial by the stain of naked yellow candlelight. With a tiny shock you see by that same light the menu designed by the world's highest-priced living artist, Andrew Wyeth. More Wyeth prints on the walls (they were once the originals but, alas, replaced after an ungrateful diner made off with "The Dory.")

The Wyeths had a hand in starting up things for the owner, Dorothy Theodore, a good friend, and you never know when you'll run into Andrew or Betsy. But there are stronger reasons for eating here than catching a glimpse of the Wyeth's with pie on their face. The steaks, for instance: "There are none better anywhere," said a rival innkeeper with real awe in his voice. (The price for such excellence seems within bounds: New York cut sirloin is $7.00; the junior, $5.00.) Duck

($5.95) is good eating too, but a few slices of mandarin orange do not a *bigarade* sauce make. With it came both brown-and-wild rice pilau *and* the inescapable baked potato with sour cream! Gulp. In addition to the greenery, the salad bar is stocked with such Pennsylvania Dutch standards as three-bean salad and pickled beets and cherry pickles. Bread is there too—hack away. For dessert, grasshopper pie, which, for beginners, is the transmogrification of the drink of the same name. It's made with *creme de menthe* on a chocolate crumb crust under glorious whipped cream that unfortunately drowns out any memory of alcohol. Then coffee, to drown the whipped cream.

Since they opened the BRANDYWINE ART MUSEUM just down the road the old guard has had a hard time elbowing a path to their favorite tables at lunchtime, and if they get there they have to sit with the rabble a long time before procuring food from the hard-pressed staff. Are crab Newburg, chicken *crêpes* and mushroom omelettes worth suffering for when you can have a quick, well-set-up sandwich or a homemade ice cream cone at the museum cafeteria? Then by all means go, except Saturday when the decision is made for you—the inn is closed for lunch—and Sunday when it's closed all day.

> Chadd's Ford Inn, *Rte. 1, Chadd's Ford, Pa. 19317. Located 21 mi. S of Phil. near Brandywine Museum. Dorothy Theodore, Prop. L—11.30-2; D—5-11. Not open for lunch Sat., closed Sun. Phone: 302-388-7361.*

Driving south of Kennett Square on U.S. 1 the scene changes without warning. Uneventful rural passages give over to a strange new nightmarish vista—acre upon acre of low-lying sheds like blind greenhouses. Not a few of them seem to be fuming in the blanched sunlight of early spring. Smoke, or is it steam?, is issuing out of chinks, cracks, door slits. More smoke is curling sinuously out of a pile of peat unloaded in front of one or another of the sheds, but the expected conflagration never comes. This is the mushroom capital of the country. The fumes are fumigation fumes. Mushroom farming, an exact science, is a spooky business.

There is a conflagration of a kind of a little farther down the road beginning at West Grove, but it's done with roses. Most people who come this way haven't come to gaze upon a lot of wan mushrooms in their strange habitats, but upon zillions of roses—crimson, garnet, white, yellow, blush pink, pink-pink, salmon and all the shades between. The greenhouses of the CONOVER-PYLE COMPANY (the Peace rose people) are open all year, and from mid-May to October visitors are welcome to come and fill the eye in the fields of STAR ROSE gardens farther down the road. For another kind of nourishment there's the beautiful old

RED ROSE INN
West Grove, Pennsylvania

It's taken a while—nearly two hundred and thirty-four years—to perfect the color of that brick. Rose red. The walks are the same brick and pick a path through a low maze of hedges to the porch. The charm of the place seeps through the very boards of the floor. Little choice objects have been set about as if absent-mindedly. Fireplaces grow like weeds (there are five down below in what is perhaps the most interesting part of the house). The inevitable expansion has been accomplished not only with taste but with talent, especially the barroom carved as it was out of the old carriage house and installed with a bar out of a fine old Philadelphia mansion.

Let no one be surprised to find a rose or two on the table in front of you, summer or winter, and mushrooms on the menu night or noon. At lunch time, mushrooms creamed on toast, mushroom omelette, a French-toasted sandwich. For dinner, sautéed mushrooms are offered as a side dish.

The Red Rose has chosen its owners wisely. The newest is himself
a chef,* a pretty good one from all accounts. Originally from Germany,
he says he has come home at last. There are no present radical plans
to change things-as-they-are, but he will expand the repertory of
steaks and has a hand-picked agent at the shore to see that he gets
the very freshest fish each day. If the new regime is responsible for
the leaping fresh broiled rockfish on this occasion you are in luck.
It comes with a side order of creamed mushrooms and yeasty little
pop-in-the-mouth rolls. Everything except the watery vegetable soup
is very well prepared. For dessert in this place where food is not —
maybe that should read *has* not — been the *raison d'être* there is a
lemon tart beyond compare made with such shocking goodies as
lemons and eggs and whipped real cream and never a pinch of cornstarch. It's made by one of the old retainers. Long may she stay at her
post.

> Red Rose Inn, *West Grove, Pa. 19390. Located in the coun-*
> *try, on U.S. 1 about 2 miles west of town. Claire & Herbie*
> *Rambold, Prop. L — noon-2.30, D — 5-9 weekdays & Sat.,*
> *noon-7 Sun. Closed Tues. Phone: 215-869-9964.*

In this favored part of the world, the minute you get off the Pike,
otherwise known as U.S. 1, you're in the country. Just like that. Some
day soon get off where you see the sign pointing the way to

THE OLD MILL
Concordville, Pennsylvania

THREE MILES LATER and out of the woods, there is the pond and here
is the mill. It's shivery to remember that this big white slab of a building built by Swedish settlers in 1682 was an historic landmark at the
time it was providing the power to grind the grain for Washington's
troops encamped down the road at Chadd's Ford. Inside, dwarfing
everything in sight is the waterwheel. It reaches up through the
ceiling to the floor above making seductive watery noises all the
while, a kind of dinner music, as it lurches around describing its arc
over and over, over and over. As you reach the dining area upstairs
there is the powerful dripping-wet shoulder of the wheel rising and
falling in the Mill Room.
Gastronomically speaking, too, you have come to a rather remarkable place, a throwback to an age of innocence before menus were
peppered with the *accent aigu* and when a sauce was something that

*Just taking over at the time of this visit and proceeding slowly, with caution.

went on ice cream. The most exotic item on the menu – and a specialty of the house – is deep-fried whole button mushrooms.

How long has it been since you read a menu that calls a chicken a chicken, a steak a steak, a pork chop a pork chop? There are seventeen such entrées, most of which are broiled. The cooking is completely without artifice so the ingredients have to be the best: there's no place to hide. Even the sweetbreads come sliced in half and broiled, unapologetically themselves, sizzling in their own juices on a pewter platter.

Accompaniments couldn't be more prosaic. Baked Idaho potatoes with you-know-what . . . succotash . . . wedge-of-lettuce salad. The owner confessed that lack of help may soon force him to add a salad bar; it would be a shame in a way.

For dessert, homemade chocolate cake, a cake of substance and spread uncertainly with old-fashioned white buttercream icing, everyone's first chocolate cake. It would not make good on the pages of *McCall's* but it *tastes* good, hang it all. The coffee could hold its own anywhere in the world.

> The Old Mill, *Brinton Lake Rd., Concordville, Pa. 19331. Located in the country, 2 mi. SW of town. Althea Upperman, Prop. D only – 5.30-9 Tues.-Fri., 5-9.30 Sat., 2-7 Sun. (except July and Aug.). Closed Mon., Thanksgiving, Christmas & month of January. Phone: 215-459-2140.*

At a quiet country crossroads-of-history not far off the Pike there's the

---

DILWORTHTOWN INN
Dilworthtown, Pennsylvania

IT'S A DELICIOUSLY illicit act, eating at Dilworthtown Inn. There you are tucked away in a room that holds only four tables . . . in the enforced intimacy of candlelight – alone at last! And 154 diners just like you (the place is, well, **jammed**) are getting the same message in **their** little semi-private rooms. **Amazing**. Amazing how they took a 200-year-old straightforward stucco'd brick tavern and by dint of sheer talent and, let's admit it at once, soup-pots full of greens, turned it into an Experience, Fireplaces in all the rooms. The glint of pewter and cut glass. Bare, burnished wood tables. Bare wood floors. Deferential waiters. This is not your ordinary rabbit's warren. If the food runs consistently behind expectations, it's not to say the food isn't good, just that it isn't *that* good: oftener than we know expectations are scaled to the price we have to pay. Also be it remembered, it's Saturday night.

Escargots bourguignonnes are excellent, worth chasing with the good house bread which is brought forth whole on a wooden plank as is the custom of the country. Watercress soup tastes more of the potato than the cress, and the veal *"Cordon Rouge,"* in spite of the laying on of ham, of cheese, of béchamel sauce, is much ado about very little. The Dilworthtown potatoes, if read correctly, are little half-baked potatoes, cut in sections with their skins on, then fried—*interesting.* All around, diners are falling happily on charcoaled entrecôtes: make a note! For dessert, you may have *crêpes Suzettes* or baked Alaska or a simple but smashing *crème caramel.* Count on $15 to $20 for dinner with drink and tip but bring your checkbook to pay for the wine. The wine list is good reading, for this is a better-than-average cellar, but you may find interesting under-$10 selections are largely a matter of history.

> Dilworthtown Inn, *Old Wilmington Pike & Britton Bridge Rds., Dilworthtown, Pa. 19380. (Mailing address: West Chester). Located S of West Chester off Rte. 202. Timothy W. McCarthy, Prop. L—11.30-2.30 Mon.-Fri., D—5.30-10 Mon.-Thurs., till 11 Fri. & Sat., 3-9 Sun. Open daily year-round. AE, BA, MC. Reservations a must: 303-399-1390.*

There aren't too many inn-inns, as distinct from motor inns, that welcome the traveling stranger. The times have made people wary . . . help is hard to get . . . coping in the kitchen consumes all available energies. "I live here too, upstairs, and I'm often alone in the house," explained one innkeeper, a widow. "How would I sleep if there were a bunch of strangers rattling down the hall?" Would she take in lodgers if she knew them? The answer comes elliptically: "I have to offer lodgings you know, in order to get a liquor license."

Realistically, if you're looking to bed down in an old inn, shaped by history and shadowy with ghosts, you would be well-advised to make friends with the owner or get a job on the premises (the help often occupy the guest rooms overhead). Most of the time the rest of us must go on down the road and put up with air conditioning, TV, swimming pools and other bedrocks of modern existence. In all of Chester county the nearest thing to an old inn where you are welcome to put up as well as eat up and drink up, is

---

MENDENHALL INN
Mendenhall, Pennsylvania

SEVERAL MANAGEMENTS AGO, this luxurious inn with its continental ways was an old lumbermill. Expanded in several directions it now reaches around and encloses an inner courtyard, a secret garden threaded by a stream visible from all the rooms. In back, the railroad tracks by the loading platform still glint in the sun and the mill stands, seemingly intact. Inside, there's not so much as a splinter to show from the old, rough days. All that's behind us now except on weekends when guests may climb upstairs to dance in the raw old Mill Room. Up among the beams and rafters it would surprise no one to see a bird or two swooping about, dazzled by the wheeling light from the chandeliers and the Hitchcock shadows sent up by galaxies of candles on the tables.

The service strives for elegance: linens, pewter serving plates, pistol-handled knives, stemmed goblets, maitre d's who bend at waist or elbow, ceremonial Caesar salads at tableside and beaucoup pyromania: there are five flambé entrees, three flambé desserts and *café brulôt* on the dinner menu. Maybe this is simply to see by . . . it's so dark in the main room you can't distinguish what's in front of you till along about dessert time when your eyes have grown used to it.

All the showmanship distracts from the food which is fine. A good lobster bisque to begin. Beef Wellington (which arrived the first time around on the far side of rare) tasteful, plump, plastered with foie gras, in a crust like good Yorkshire pudding. (But elegance grows a bit strained before the universal baked potato in the super size, and the salad, à la carte, was smaller and less interesting than the ones that usually accompany entrées unasked.) Dessert, a toplofty frosted raspberry soufflé, comes floating above the thinnest of wine glasses, lovely to look at and lovely to demolish.

The rooms with their view of the garden are a little more luxurious than most, the towels a bit bigger, and the formica around the sink is marble. Maybe modern living is not all bad. In the morning a continental breakfast is available in the dining room: the miniature *schnecken* are worth getting up early for and the coffee is fiery.

Mendenhall Inn, *Kennett Pike (Rte. 52), Mendenhall, Pa. 19357. 1 mi. S of Baltimore Pike (Rte. 1). Arthur Hastings, Gen. Mgr. Open Tues.-Sat. for lunch and dinner . . . Sunday buffet. Closed Mon. and two weeks in July. Lodgings. AE, CB, MC. Information, reservations: 215-388-7676.*

PILGRIMAGE TO

COVENTRYVILLE

IN A CLASS BY ITSELF, tucked away in the northwest corner of Chester county all by itself, is an inn mentioned always with a certain awe followed by the word "Go!":

COVENTRY FORGE INN
Coventryville, Pennsylvania

WEST OF *Les Frères Troisgros* and south of *La Côte Basque,* this is as close as you're likely to come to topflight French food. It's close enough to warrant the drive, a long haul. Coventryville, saved by a swerve of the road from the fate overtaking too many charming little towns, could be a tiny village in France waiting to be discovered. The inn is on a rise above it, a stucco'd stone house looking out over a long reach of countryside that can't have changed much since 1717 when the inn was built. The long, light-filled glassy porch brings the view right up to your table or you can eat in one of the small candle-lit tavern-like rooms with its sense of cozy familiarity with the past.

At the first inhalation of the *feuilleté d'escargots Champenoise* (snails in puff-pastry shells swathed in a mysterious miraculous sauce—the recipe like so many others come from the owners' last trip to France) you begin to relax. This is the real thing. The sauce

172

does what a sauce should: tells you more about what you're eating, and the feuilleté is a crumbling edifice that melts on the tongue. By comparison, *coquilles St. Jacques* are a letdown with a *soupçon* too much salt besides. Another appetizer for which Coventry Forge is famous is the *truite au bleu*, where the trout is knocked out then cast into boiling rapids—not for the niece of a vegetarian though you are assured the trout never knows what hit it. Among the entrées is steak *au poivre verte,* the first time you have come upon this glamorous new spice. Gentler but twangier than black pepper it is muted still further with cream and port and has a way with a fine piece of steak which this is. But add to it the house potatoes (cooked in cream with a whoosh of garlic) and asparagus *hollandaise,* and you may wish wistfully for the plain rack of lamb or nice, naked soft shell crabs or the calf's liver *persillé* this night. There *is* such a thing as too much cream. Salad is a mystery. It isn't mentioned on the menu and when you ask about it the waitress with a secret smile advises you to wait and see if there's room for it. There isn't. Owner Wally Callahan, is an oenophile in earnest, one who knows that salad is the enemy. For dessert, fresh strawberries, four unbelievable peaks rising above a pale yellow lake of Grand Marnier sauce. The espresso that follows is a fine jolt—just what is needed—and there's a whole potful.

Perfection is no accident. The chef was trained by the apprenticeship system in France and by osmosis at Coventry Forge side by side with the talented cook-and-owner. A local baker comes in each day to make puff pastry and babas and sour dough bread.

The wine cellar has quite a reputation that's been a-building for years, but a lot of good that will do you for the prices are today's toplofty prices. Still, a Chateaux la-tour-de-Mons Soussons-Margaux '67 ($6.50 the half-bottle) is worth every *sous.*

To help preserve the purity of the village, the Callahans have recently bought another old house, setting it up for sybaritic, well-heeled guests. Baths, bidets and continental breakfasts are included for your money.

> Coventry Forge Inn, *Coventryville Rd., Coventryville, Pa. (Mailing address: R.D. 2, Pottstown, Pa. 19464). Located just off Rte. 23, 6 mi. SE of Pottstown. Wallis Callahan, Prop. D only—5.30-9 weekdays, 5-10 Sat. Closed Sun. (Nov. thru Apr. also closed Mon.). On vacation week before Labor Day and for a month beginning day before Christmas. Reservations a must: 215-469-6222.*

FEASTING IN
FAGLEYSVILLE

SOMEWHERE IN MONTGOMERY COUNTY is a red brick hotel leftover from the middle of the last century but there is nothing else provincial about the

FAGLEYSVILLE
COUNTRY HOTEL
Gilbertsville, Pennsylvania

To BE SO FAR off the beaten track . . . to run an ambitious restaurant in a town like Fagleysville whose postal address is Gilbertsville on a pike whose name is kept a dark secret from travelers you have to be good or be damned or be damned good.

The Gleasons are amateurs in the best sense of the word. Inspired amateurs. It was just nine or ten years ago Jack Gleason opened up a country tap room where he could do what he like to do best—relax and talk to people. A little later Phyllis Gleason began to do the thing she does best—cook. Why *here*? he's often asked by his customers. "Because I like it here," he answers with an enigmatic smile.

174

The menu is clumsily typed. Selections leap wildly back and forth from cocotte to wok. Too experimental? Subtract two points. A dish of *"fruits de la mer"* is described as "cohered with a cream sauce." Subtract ½ point. On the other hand, the menu urges a Kir (white burgundy with a splash of cassis) or vermouth cassis before dinner or Lillet, instead of, say, a Harvey Wallbanger. Add three points. Then the food comes and the nonsense-game is over. A delicate, dreamy watercress soup. Score. The *duck à la Fagleysville*, is duck unmasked. Defatted and deboned, it's so tender it can be eaten with merely the prod of a fork. The flavor is inscrutable *orientale* — no oranges, cherries, plums, kumquats or pineapple to hide the truth. Trout Japanese-style is an Idaho trout that meets a beautiful fate: it's stuffed to the gills with a hot salad of springy, chewy, crunchy vegetables (scallions, green pepper, celery, mushrooms) and broiled in a wrapper of bacon. Either entrée will help console you for sacrificing the *entrecôte de beouf Madrid* (sirloin strip with a walnut-anchovy-garlic sauce) and the *lobster Conil* (flambé'd with Pernod in a béchamel sauce). Just toy with the scalloped potatoes and the broccoli in lemon butter, and save yourself for two marvelous house specialties, South Korean onion wedges marinated and broiled and an off-beat salad — romaine, orange and onion in a good French dressing available à la carte. You may want to concentrate on the bread (French) and butter (extraordinary . . . it tastes like the fresh-washed butter of Switzerland)

and drink dessert—Irish coffee. If it's half as good as the pot of beady brown espresso—! Desserts run to ice cream and a mousse; pecan delight with its dab of vanilla ice cream is a high school treat, and doesn't belong in this classy company.

At the next table a "chef" from Howard Johnson is wining and dining with great éclat all by himself, as if this were a last supper. He's come to the right place.

> Fagleysville Country Hotel, *Swamp Pike Rd. between Limerick (Rte. 422) and Boyertown (Rte. 100). (Mailing address: RD 1, Gilbertsville, Pa. 19525.) Jack Gleason, Prop. Open daily year-round. L—noon-2, D—from 6 Mon.-Fri., D only Sat. from 5, Sun. from 4. AE. Reservations urged: 215-323-1425.*

XII.

WAY DOWN SOUTH
IN SOUTH JERSEY

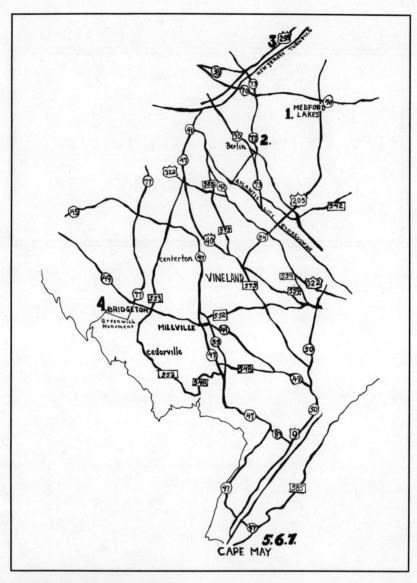

1. **MEDFORD LAKES LODGE**
2. **LUCIEN'S OLD TAVERN**
3. **YE OLDE CENTERTON INN**
4. **THE BAIT BOX**
5. **CHALFONTE HOTEL**
6. **WATSON'S MERION INN**
7. **THE WASHINGTON INN**

THE PINES

WOULD IT SURPRISE ANYONE to learn that the third smallest, most densely populated state in the nation has a wilderness and near-wilderness area almost as large as Yosemite? From Lakewood it spreads south to the Mullica River and westward halfway across the state. This is the region known, perhaps unfortunately, as the PINE BARRENS. From a car window all that can be seen is whitish sandy soil and mile upon mile of stunted pine and oak. It's boring, boring, boring—step on to the gas. No intimation of the remarkable botanical treasures within. Few signs of the hundreds of miles of river and stream and bog, the mysterious waters that sluice through the riotous, jungle-like growth . . . waters always seen through dark glasses for these are cedar waters, water the color of tea.

These same tea-colored waters, the last of the potable small rivers and streams in the East, occasionally parted now by a canoe or pinged by a dragonfly or a frog, was once the source of the raw ore that was the basis of the early iron industry. Bog iron it's called, and they raked it up from the banks with cranberry forks. Company towns where iron-masters lived like feudal lords, and workers, slave and non-slave alike, worked twelve-hour days and seven-day weeks sprang up in the Pines; they provided the muscle that won a Revolution and a War of 1812. They also provided the building blocks—the pots, the pans, the stoves, the pipes—the new nation had to have.

Public transit companies serving the area: Bus from N.Y.C.—Garden State Coachways (Medford Lakes), Lincoln Transit (Cape May); Bus from Phila.—Transport of New Jersey (Berlin, Cape May); Train from Phila.—Pennsylvania-Reading Seashore Lines (Cape May).

179

There were 30 such towns in Monmouth and Ocean counties alone. Gone now, except for the ghost towns—a rehabilitated village like ALLAIRE or BATSTO or a stand of catalpa trees writhing over the fate of MARTHA FURNACE. New Jersey is said to have more ghost towns than in all the old West. Most have been fed to the forests . . . recycled nature's way. Ironically the steel industry* with its pop-world landscape re-established across the river from Bordentown, has made a come-back in this part of the world. But for over a hundred years—after the source of supply began to thin out in the bogs and, more devastatingly, better grade ore had been located in Pennsylvania—the iron furnaces were cold. Fires were frequent in the Pines, fanning the beginning of the end. At ATSION there is a pretty little lake of dark soft cedar water to picnic by, swim in, just across the highway from the old town with its formidable mansion and company store, its vaguely disquieting aura of an unfinished time.

Should you be looking for the site of the former Etna Furnace you will find few clues in and around MEDFORD LAKES. Starting up in 1930 as a summer colony, it was built entirely of logs on the ashes of the old feudal iron town at the entrance to the pine barrens. North of town is typical South Jersey farmland while just across the bridge it

*U.S. Steel's Fairless Works.

is sandy as the seashore underfoot and useless for cultivation. Iron-master Charles Read's home is all that remains of Etna; the rest of the village is the work of a later entrepreneur. Even the church and its belfry is made of logs as are the stores lined up along a curving streetfront. Grandfather of them all is

---

MEDFORD LAKES LODGE
Medford Lakes, New Jersey

THERE IS NOTHING HUMBLE about this log cabin. It was built on the grand scale, a princely hunting lodge worthy of an early iron king or present chairman of the board. Every log in it was sawed by hand, since there was no electricity or gas-powered equipment in the area when the village was going up. A stone fireplace, said to be the largest ever built, mounts one wall, and a huge clock with a six-foot pendulum is built into the chimney. There are trophies of the hunt on the walls, and Indian insignia and artifacts representing the tribes that a few centuries back roamed this region. The ceiling seems very far away. It is . . . 75 feet away. Rooms, simple, rustic, but not too rustic for private baths and reading lamps by the bed, are off the gallery.

There are wild roses on the tables in the dining room and a professional chef in the kitchen. The new proprietor is caught up in the legend of the Pines, and like the chef, moved here for the rich life, the hunting, the fishing, in a community where "ducks and children go first." It is very informal and relaxed. The chef declines to be involved in any cook-off. Fish is his specialty, crab his passion (he is a Marylander, after all); only the finest lump crab goes into the Crab Imperial. His chauvinism extends to local vegetables in season, but local blueberries can't rescue the pie—opt for ice cream.

The lodge and town are unique Americana, tomorrow's historical preservations. Guests of the hotel have a beachfront on Medford Lake which like the twenty-some finger lakes in the area is mostly private. See for yourself what it's like to swim in cedar water, golden ale in the shallows, dark ale in the deeps. For the best such swimming you must push into the pine country and try LAKE OSWEGO in Penn State Forest, once a cranberry bog, now a 90-acre swimming hole.

Medford Lakes Lodge, *Stokes Road, Medford Lakes, N.J. 08088. Located 2½ mi. S of Medford Circle on Rte. 541. Harold J. Budd, Prop. Open all year. L—11.30-2.30 Tues.-Fri., till 10 Sat., 2-8 Sun. Closed Mon. Lodgings. Reservations weekends: 609-654-4034.*

When you reel off the names of certain South Jersey towns it sounds like a kind of folk poetry. Names like Sweetwater and Mizpah and Peahala, names like Oriental and Hi-Nella and tell-it-like-it-is Bivalve. Then there are the ghost towns names: Double Trouble and Mount Misery, Batsto ("steam bath" in Swedish) . . . Arney's Mount . . . Ong's Hat. But none is lovelier to roll on the tongue than Long-a-Coming, now known as "Berlin." (**There's** a name that sounds like a town all right, Berlin. Berlin)

Long-a-Coming was a convenient stop for the riders of the stage on the rough back-country road between Camden and May's Landing. One of the taverns that would have greeted you then is still going strong. Local citizens from Glassboro to Mt. Holly agree the best food in South Jersey is to be found at

---

LUCIEN'S OLD TAVERN
Berlin, New Jersey

THINGS HAVE CHANGED in the last two centuries to be sure. This little ole tavern isn't so little anymore, and you need a knowledgable guide—maybe an on-site dig—to separate the old sticks and stones from the shiny new additions. Speaking of ghosts, Lucien still greets guests as they enter, smiling from a portrait on the wall, and from beyond the grave still dictates the menus and the recipes. A good restaurateur has to be egoist or despot. Lucien, it appears, was a bit of both. He left the old place to his employees who own and operate it as if he were there.

One of the traditions at Lucien's is Nova Scotia lobster—one can forgive much for the sake of this supreme luxury. Jersey cranberry juice (also on the menu) may be the equal of Massachusetts', but the Jersey lobster is not in the same league as lobsters that marinate in colder waters. And Nova Scotian waters are *cold.*

It's been a while since you've come across old-fashioned *fresh* lobster salad, sweet as the sea is salt. You'd like to eat enough to hold you against the long, lobsterless summers-to-come, but—impossible as it seems—there is simply too much. (Rarer than too much lamb on a lamb chop bone or too much ice cream in a soda is too much lobster.)

Allergic? There are consolations. The roast beef is a high and mighty slab, the undeniable favorite of the staff. They shrug when you order something else, as if you had gone against a law of nature, as if they had tried but failed to convince a stubborn child. Stubborn child, a long-shot gambler, orders fried oysters with crabmeat salad instead, or fried scallops with chicken salad, or more conservatively Baltimore deviled crab made with lump meat. S.C., though burned many times, might gamble again and win on the item listed as "Really Home-Made Pies."

You may have to do some forgiving. The cherrystones are briny. The vichyssoise exudes the peculiar strength of overcooked onion. *Crême brulée* turns out to be old friend *crême caramel*, not *brulée* at all, the suave cold creamy riches under the thin crackly caramelized crust.

The most old-fashioned aspect of Lucien's is the service, with the accent on formal white linen rather than lobster bibs, appetizers and cold soups and relishes sunk in quantities of ice, black-suited waiters skating between tables, working as if they own the place. Apparently they do.

Before you leave, check the bar stools on their heavily wrought wrought iron bases, but it won't do any good to make an offer. It's been tried.

> Lucien's Old Tavern, *81 W. White Horse Pike, Berlin, N.J. 08009. Located on Rte. 30 about 18 mi. from center of Philadelphia. Frank Selby, Maitre'd. L — noon-2; D — 4-10 Mon.- Sat., 2-10 Sun. À la carte anytime till 1 or 2 am. Closed Christmas Eve and Day, July 4th, Labor Day. Phone: 609-767-0285 or 9720 or 9733.*

```
┌─────────────────────────────────────────────┐
│                                               │
│   BACKWATER AND                               │
│                                               │
│   TIDEWATER                                   │
│                                               │
└─────────────────────────────────────────────┘
```

GEORGIA GETS THE CREDIT, but Jersey peaches are the apogee of peach. Ask anyone who's ever bitten into a rich streaming yellow Sun High or Blake or the more subtle and flowery white Hale (actually not white at all but palest green with a touch of rouge and smelling like a rose). Hundreds of acres of peach orchards flow into one another down in the plains of South Jersey, a lather of pink in late April and waiting at the end of one heavenly lane there's

```
┌─────────────────────────────────────────────┐
│                                               │
│   YE OLDE CENTERTON INN                       │
│                    Centerton, New Jersey      │
│                                               │
└─────────────────────────────────────────────┘
```

CENTERTON, NEW JERSEY, *is* Centerton Inn. A pre-Revolutionary stage stop when this was the main route from Cumberland County to Great Egg Harbor it's now more often the end-of-the-road for the people who come for a sense of communion with the past and, of course, the food — in that order.

Centerton Inn as we know it is the chef d'oeuvre of William Sedgwick who thirty years ago bought a simple South Jersey tavern like so many that line the roads with their "Pizza . . . Package Goods" signs and transformed it into a refuge from future shock. He filled it full of mellow paintings by early American artists, with old clocks and docu-

184

ments and ceiling lamps, a very personal collection of overwhelming charm. Going from room to room and inching up the stairs where still more dining areas open up this way and that, as if by random, is like going on a treasure hunt.

The new owner kept it all for he understands their value, as well as the value of serving good food. As he says, anybody who comes here has to come here from somewhere else – there is no (well, almost no) Centerton.

If he and his chef don't understand the subtle requirements of soups and sauces – and they don't – they make up for it in other directions, going way out of the way to procure excellence in meats and fish. Centerton Inn is famous for seafood platters which include *sautéed* soft-shell crab and *fresh* flounder, fried oysters, shrimp and lobster tail. Star, too, calf's liver and onions, a rare delicacy when cooked right. The house salad, picked up with Parmesan and is-it-celery seed?, is above par, the French fries, are professional, and the rolls irresistible. Rum cake, a specialty, wasn't ready this noonday, but it's hand-wrought unlike some other offerings and should be worth waiting upon. It's rumored to have rum in it!

> Ye Olde Centerton Inn, *Rtes. 540 & 553, Centerton, N.J. 08318. Centerton is at a crossroads 12 mi. S of Glassboro. Robert & Samuel Garrison, Prop. L – noon-2; D – 5-9, 2-9 Sun. Closed Mon. AE, DC. Phone: 609-358-3201.*

If the Delaware Bay had been called (with equal logic) New Jersey Bay it might not fall so trippingly off the tongue, but it would have helped New Jersey's identity crisis. The same bay that wets one shore wets the other, impartially. Both are fringed deeply with miles of salt marshes that part to let the creeks pass by, and the birds, insects, beasts that find refuge in the marshgrass make no distinction. This, too, is tidewater country.

Two hundred years ago much of what is now marsh is said to have been farmland. Boats as large as 1000 tons were built on Dennis Creek near the pretty, pleasing New England-like village of DENNIS-VILLE; they were made from the cedar mined in the nearby swamps and valued for its resistance to water after the centuries of lying about in the muck. South Jersey, once a seafloor, is said to be sinking, and some of the same forces that buried the cedars have been filling in Dennis Creek, ploughing fields under water and nibbling at the shoreline.

Two hundred years ago when the bay was a main access route to Philadelphia, PORT ELIZABETH (a tiny landing now), SALEM and GREEN-WICH were shipping ports of no little importance. Greenwich a smaller indigenous form of Williamsburg, appears to be keeping itself in readiness for a replay of the eighteenth century. 100-foot wide Greate Street is roofed with trees and lined with "towne houses" . . . except for the paving and a lone gasoline pump, that weed of the present, it seems to have been preserved by some invisible mist off the Cohansey. Several of the houses are the fancy patterned brickwork that crops up often in South Jersey—herringbone- or checkerboard, occasionally signed and dated on the gable end like a cross-stitch sampler. Descendents of the builders and of the lawless "rebels" who, dressed in Indian paint and feathers, held a flaming "tea party" on this wide, placid, imperturbable avenue a year after the one in Boston are still living in some of them. There's a biannual house tour in the spring.

Yes, go out of your way to wind down to Greenwich by road or, even, plough up* the Cohansey by boat. You needn't go away hungry either merely because there's no restaurant in town. At Hancock Harbor in nearby Bacon's Neck there's a local institution called

THE BAIT BOX
Greenwich, New Jersey

WHY THIS LITTLE painted shack on the Inland waterway, hemmed in between a marine supply store, a boat yard and a dock? The best crab cakes in the world, that's why. *Including* Maryland. Furthermore, the staff is glad to share the recipe with you since it is unlikely that many will care to copy it; 98% tender sweet lumpy fresh crabmeat bound up in a teensy plash of mayonnaise. The crust that gets it all together, crisply, tenderly, is corn meal crumbs. You might as well know the whole truth—it's Golden Dipt corn meal crumbs. (The cook, one of the local women, takes a seat at the counter behind a platter of golden brown fritters—corn? apple? they make both—and deftly demolishes them.) The cole slaw is crisp and juicy, *today's*.

For dessert there is a superb banana cream pie assembled in the back room moments before serving so it will be at its prime, the short crust crisp and blistery, bananas dead-ripe, the custard cool and creamy. No cornstarch or flour or arrowroot thicken it—just eggs and money. As you are putting it away your head is already plotting what to order second time around. The Fisherman's Wharf crab and shrimp chowder, perhaps. Then a wedge, two wedges maybe, of Old Greenwich clam pie (clam pie lives in a personal pantheon of all-time favorite dishes). It wins, but not without a short struggle, over fresh-caught fish of the day. As to dessert, the homemade cake with or without the homemade orange sherbet seems to be ahead. Then, again, there's the apple fritters to consider. . . .

*Or down the Cohansey which is navigable all the way from Bridgeton.

The Bait Box at Hancock's Harbor, *Bacon's Neck, N.J.* *(Mailing address: R.D. 2, Bridgeton, N.J. 08302.) Located 8 mi. S of Bridgeton near town of Greenwich on the Cohansey River. Direction signs from Bridgeton and Greenwich. Joseph Hancock & Ed Du Bois, Prop. Open during season (mid-June thru Labor Day) 5-8 Tues.-Fri. for dinner. On Sat. from 12.30-8, till 7 Sun. Closed Mon., Nov. thru March, and Labor Day thru 1st weekend Nov. Sat. & Sun. only. Gulf card. For parties over 4, reservations needed: 609-455-2610.*

CAPE MAY –

GINGERBREAD-

BY-THE-SEA

LONG AGO – long before Cape May had become the preeminent resort in America – the Kechemeche Indians were summering on these shores and whales gamboled at the mouth of Delaware Bay as buffalo did on the Western plains.* That was the first Golden Age.

Then came Captain Mey who left his name, followed by the whalers who came and went with the tides of fortune, and in 1680 William Penn who almost created his City of Brotherly Love at nearby Town Bank, a town that was literally swallowed up by the sea some time later.**

The first white tourists were Philadelphians, conveyed by sail, then by steamer on regular packet boats. They came for their "constitution" (nothing so frivolous as fun), were urged not to dip in the sea too often (two or three times a week was considered consistent with good health), and slept in a barnlike dormitory partitioned with a curtain, men on one side, women on the other. Congress Hall, three

---

*The Indians would put up temporary shelters and feast on fruits of the sea in vast quantities till the shells piled up high as the dunes. It was the Indian, apparently, who braved the first oyster and downed the first clam and showed the world how. They would string oysters and mussels on twigs and smoke them in little huts, and carry these trophies back on the long homeward trek at the end of the summer.
**In a mere twenty-year span (1804-24) the sea ingested three miles of the Cape, lighthouses and all, according to Commodore Stephen Decatur, a frequent visitor.

stories high with partitioned rooms for 100 guests, was considered much too grand in 1816 when it was built, but it ushered in the second Golden Age.

In the 1850's, statesmen and society flocked here, particularly southern society; Cape May is the South, it must be remembered, dropping 55 miles below a projection of the Mason-Dixon line . . . on a level with Washington, D.C. There was a procession of statesmen and Presidents: Pierce, Buchanan, and Henry Clay and a President-to-be, A. Lincoln, and wife.

Bands played in the grand hotels, glittering carriages raked the sands of the wide beach, gentlemen took off their dueling pistols only to plough into the sea, and plantations were won and lost in an afternoon at the casinos.

Then the Civil War came, ending the southern occupation long enough to break the habit, and in '78 the hotel district was leveled by fire. Despite more Presidential visits — Grant . . . Arthur . . . Benjamin Harrison, whose summer capital it was — society turned elsewhere and excursionists were carried by train to points further north. Cape May wrapped in dignity and beauty and quiet was saved — for *us*.

Instant nostalgia? Come along the seawalk for a promenade to the madding odors of salt air and homemade candy such as disappeared thirty years back. No hustlers. No honky-tonk. Do the waves only *seem* curlier? the water warmer? Come along the tree-canopied streets. 281 Victorian buildings are strung out like lacey valentines from the past, spared* so far from the insatiable laws of economics and fire. Along the ocean, motels sleek and sleazy are one by one by one replacing the grand old wood-and-wicker hotels in a misguided attempt to imitate jazzier Wildwood further north, but step around the corner (*any corner*) and find the old dowager behind the pink althea bushes rocking on her carpenter's lace porch.

At the CHALFONTE HOTEL she can be seen at her most rococo, columns, arches, balconies forming an intricate cage and an ever-changing play of light and shadow. Built in 1876 by Henry W. Sawyer, the carpenter responsible for many of Cape May's virtuoso Victorians, the hotel is owned and operated by a crusty southern *dame* in her seventies and patronized primarily by Virginians** who come back year after year to a kind of ongoing houseparty . . . who *swear* by the spoonbread and confide that the food is the best in town. But

---

*Much of old Cape May has been officially designated as an Historic District by the National Register of Historic Places.

**The southern occupancy is somewhat ironic, for Henry Sawyer, Union soldier and a cause célèbre in his time, was nearly executed by Confederate soldiers, in a "lottery of death" when he was picked to die for the unrelated killing of two Confederate officers.

on the weekend before the Fourth with the paint not yet dried, the rugs not yet down, the screens not in, and more importantly Dorothy-the-cook not yet installed this cannot be verified. . . .

At CAPE MAY POINT people still scoop up pebbles in search of Cape May "diamonds," clear round polished pieces of quartz becoming more elusive than Captain Kidd's buried treasure. In the spring and the fall, birdwatchers flock here to stare at the spectacle of sky darkened by the passage of birds. The Cape, which has a year-round bird sanctuary, is also directly on the Atlantic Flyway; 180 varieties have been spotted on a single weekend. During an October northwester, there aren't enough roofs, riggings, telephone lines, trees to hold them all; latecomers must land on the boardwalk, covering it, and onto shoulders of watchers.

If all this sea air is making you hungry, grab a bag of coconut bars or pudgy chocolate-covered marshmallows and get in line. With relatively few good restaurants in town, lines are always long. Out of season, crowds are thinner but the lines are even longer, for most places are closed following the migration back to school of the sunny, summer kids who make up the staffs. Since you're in for it, the best line to find yourself in from May through September is the one that leads to

---

WATSON'S MERION INN
Cape May, New Jersey

A TURN-OF-THE-CENTURY TAVERN built after the fire of '78, from the street it looks like just another private period house. The food, when it comes, is worth the wait. Regional and traditional dishes such as baked, stuffed pork chops, old-fashioned chicken pot pie, lobster Newburg — they change from day to day — have a place of honor on the menu. Though not a fish house, the owner goes down to the wharf each day for the day's catch. Tonight, bluefish or flounder. For the rare highly prized drumfish you must come between May and mid-June.

The fast is broken with a quartet of relishes that include a lively slaw, with a tray of international breads, and a bright salad. The fish, stuffed flounder, is wrapped over backfin crab, is broiled to the correct fraction of a second, is *superb* — no relation to the flash-frozen version by the same name. The inn's whipped potatoes smack of cream. Somebody back there knows exactly what he's doing — and *cares*. The inn does its own baking. Old-fashioned strawberry shortcake is so old-fashioned that the strawberries are fresh and the whipped cream is whipped cream (not whipped whip) and there's a lot of it. It's served in a kind of uplifted soupbowl and swimming in crushed strawberries. Later in the season, substitute fresh peaches or blueberries. Coffee is a smash.

To lure you here earlier, there's a $2.95 entree offered each evening between five and six. It's a safe guess it isn't the 16-ounce sirloin but it's also a safe guess that it's the best bargain on the Cape. Between five and six you could inspect the paintings close-up, like the portrait of the pheasant which came from Texas Guinan's and the black and white period prints, magazine illustrations, circa 1919, in the bar. And more.

> Watson's Merion Inn, *106 Decatur St., Cape May, N.J. 08204. Located in mid-Cape May, between beach and Mall. Warren & Eivor Watson, Prop. D — 5-10 daily June-Sept. Open weekends in May and daily (except Thurs.) in Sept. Bar till??* Lodgings. *No reservations accepted. Phone: 609-884-8363.*

For breakfast, the OCEAN DECK that sits directly over the water when the tide's in, has splendid three-egg omlettes, waffles, pancakes, and a vacuum jug of coffee all your own. Or come for lunch and have the steamers. For dinner there's no fresher fish on the Cape. It's just that they lock the place tight the day after Labor Day and you can't get back in till a few minutes before July 4th. Another good lunch spot is KAHN'S UGLY MUG ON THE MALL. You can't do better than a round of raw clams or oysters floated along on icy beer. Sandwiches and salads are also available.

Among all the architectural belles on the streets of Cape May you might easily miss

THE WASHINGTON INN
Cape May, New Jersey

THAT WOULD BE A MISTAKE. This earlier, strait-laced Victorian screened by two giant crytopmeria in the front yard is one of an ever-diminishing number of traditional inns in this section of the country still operating in the traditional way. Guests of The Washington Inn needn't eat and run. Poor buffeted travelers, *stay*.

A private house until 1940, it still *feels* like a private house. Every inch looks petted. Every stick in it was chosen by a trained eye. It's not unusual when someone hits the piano in the parlor, for all to fall to and sing, beginning with Ruth Kane. The Kanes like it here. The feeling is contagious. The guest rooms are Ruth Kane's garden and each one is like a room prepared for a beloved, long-awaited visitor. Some of the most charming effects come from family hand-me-downs, like the Victorian print on Patterson silk in one of the rooms or like the old glass chandelier in the hall. One room is wicker, wall-to-wall, another occupied by a canopied bed, another by two spool beds. All have showers or baths.

The food is admittedly modest. Happily, so are the prices. Approach more ambitious undertakings like French-fried mushrooms or cherry cheesecake with caution, but note that the fish is fresh. In Cape May that *means* something. On an evening when the kids are tired, it will do very nicely. Breakfasts on the screened porch can be as long and leisurely as you like, punctuated with cups of first-class coffee.

In a local antique shop you come upon a beautiful old secretary with a "sold" sign on it, sold in fact to people named Kane. Wonder where they're going to put *that*?

Washington Inn, 801 Washington St., Cape May, N.J. 08204. Located within a short walk of the Mall. Donald & Ruth Kane, Prop. Open May 15-Sept. 15. Tues.-Sun. for bkfst., dinner. Dining room is closed Mon. Lodgings. Reservations: 609-884-7293.

INNS WITH LODGINGS

BEEKMAN ARMS, *Rhinebeck, N.Y.*
OLD DROVER'S INN, *Dover Plains, N.Y.*
MOHONK MOUNTAIN HOUSE, *New Paltz, N.Y.*
DePUY'S CANAL (HOUSE) TAVERN, *High Plains, N.Y.*

THE ELMS, *Ridgefield, Conn.*
HOPKINS INN, *New Preston, Conn.*
KILVAROOK INN, *Litchfield, Conn.*

CHESTER INN, *Chester, N.J.*
SILVER SPRINGS FARM, *Flanders, N.J.*

AMERICAN HOTEL, *Freehold, N.J.*
RUMSON HOTEL, *Rumson, N.J.*
MOLLY PITCHER INN, *Red Bank, N.J.*

PEACOCK INN, *Princeton, N.J.*
NASSAU INN, *Princeton, N.J.*

HOTEL FAUCHÈRE, *Milford, Penn.*
CLIFF PARK INN, *Milford, Penn.*
REBER'S, *Barryville, N.Y.*

HENRYVILLE HOUSE, *Henryville, Penn.*
THE PUMP HOUSE, *Canadensis, Penn.*

LOGAN INN, *New Hope, Penn.*
LAMBERTVILLE HOUSE, *Lambertville, N.J.*
BLACK BASS HOTEL, *Lumberville, Penn.*

1740 HOUSE, *Lumberville, Penn.*
THE GOLDEN PHEASANT, *Erwinna, Penn.*
WASHINGTON CROSSING INN, *Washington
  Crossing, Penn.*
TEMPERANCE HOUSE, *Newtown, Penn.*

HAAG'S HOTEL, *Shartlesville, Penn.*
TULPEHOCKEN MANOR FARM, *Myerstown, Penn.*
HOTEL BETHLEHEM, *Bethlehem, Penn.*
GENERAL SUTTER INN, *Lititz, Penn.*

HOTEL DU PONT, *Wilmington, Del.*
MENDENHALL INN, *Mendenhall, Penn.*

MEDFORD LAKES LODGE, *Medford Lakes, N.J.*
CHALFONTE HOTEL, *Cape May, N.J.*
WATSON'S MERION INN, *Cape May, N.J.*
THE WASHINGTON INN, *Cape May, N.J.*